I
LOVE
DIN

I Love Type Series
Volume Four

M000209125

Published
by Viction:ary

Edited & Designed
by TwoPoints.Net

Interview with Mr. DIN
Albert-Jan Pool

When you shared a cab with Erik Spiekermann to the San Francisco Airport in 1994 and he proposed you to design FF DIN for FontShop International, were you already interested in German constructed type design?

Erik and I had both visited ATypI San Francisco, during the ride he mentioned that he had some ideas for typefaces in his drawers. He suggested that I'd come by take a look at those in order to see if I could work on them. A few weeks later I visited Erik at MetaDesign in Berlin and here he proposed the idea of expanding OCR-B and DIN into type families. Also the design quality should be improved, so that they would not just stay sort of funny but also become usable. Until that day I had not been interested in constructed type design as such. When I studied in The Hague, Gerrit Noordzij was my teacher and he argued that "the guys at the Bauhaus" might have done interesting things when it comes to architecture and design, but that their contributions to type design did not have any relevance when it comes to usable forms, let alone readability.

ATypI San Francisco
1994 T-Shirt

In the early nineties one of URW's distributors asked me whether the type studio could add some weights to DIN Mittelschrift. He envisioned that such a family could be marketed successfully. I rejected the project, arguing that it would not make sense to put a typeface design on the market with a quality that is obviously lower than Univers, Helvetica, Akzidenz Grotesk and many others.

You were born and raised in the Netherlands. Coming from a very rich typographic culture and having studied at the Royal Academy of Arts in The Hague do you think you had a different approach on the design of FF DIN?

The common expectation would have been that from a "The Hague point of view", I would have come up with the proposal to throw away DIN and design something decent. That does not fully do justice to what we were taught there. Gerrit Noordzij stated that from a type designer's point of view he considered typefaces such as Bembo and Plantin as poorly revived historical masterpieces but from a typographer's

Gerrit Noordzij and his
favorite teaching arti-
fact: the black board at
the Royal Academy of
Arts in the Hague.
© 1981 by Ronald
Schmets

point of view they could perform excellently. At The Hague we were not just taught to judge typefaces on their design alone, we mainly learned how to look at them in order to see how they would perform typographically. This is different from the way "type" was taught in the German art academies those days though. Drawing type was something for sign painters and they were not taught at art academies but at vocational schools. At art academies one would find highly skilled calligraphers who rather considered themselves as artists instead of craftsmen. Calligraphy and type design were considered completely independent disciplines. When it came to type design at all, they'd tell faux stories about Baskerville imitating copperplate engraving and Bodoni having constructed his typefaces with compass and rulers. Futura was usually explained by quoting Paul Standard, who said "Geometry can produce legible letters, but art alone makes them beautiful." Logos were designed using existing typefaces "with proven quality" such as Helvetica anyway ... They did not really want to get involved with type design, let alone with computers. The type designers of those days had somehow accepted that with software such as Ikarus one could more easily create final artwork, but even interpolation was often considered as an evil invention. In The Hague the attitude was different, Gerrit Noordzij had seen how his student Petr van Blokland quickly managed to make his computers do what he wanted them to. Through ATypI Gerrit had got in contact with Peter Karow, the inventor of Ikarus. This resulted in URW digitizing and interpolating Gerrit's two squares with which he proved that most typefaces can easily be classified into only two groups. From then, these squares were the basic illustration of his theories on writing, type design and classification in The Hague. With the three-dimensional version of 1985, also known as the Typographic Cube or Universe, the purple "transitional" classes were integrated. Gerrit redrew the eight corners and Petr van Blokland digitized and interpolated the intermediate characters. In The Hague we learned how to handle a broad and a pointed nib in order to see how writing affects the main stylistic directions in type design, but at the same time Gerrit encouraged us to explore the new digital technologies. He envisioned that his synthesis of writing and digital type would help us designers to regain complete control over our work again. The present situation tells us that he was right with that.

After my studies I have been working as a type director at Scangraphic and URW for several years. Here I worked on a lot of typefaces that were being digitized and adapted for the pro-

Expansion or pointed-nib based contrast (Didonic / Modern)
© 1976 by Gerrit Noordzij

Translation or broad-nib based contrast (Garalde / Old Style)
© 1976 by Gerrit Noordzij

Fortunately Peter Karow recognized that the type department was not to blame for that. He generously allowed me to work on my first type designs URW Linear and Imperial. So when Erik came up with the idea of designing FF DIN I was probably the right guy in the right place at the right time. He has a nose for such things!

Since 2004 you are investigating constructed sans serifs designed in Germany. You are even writing a doctoral thesis, supervised by Gerard Unger, about this subject. Constructed typefaces were designed as well in other countries. Why did you concentrate your research on Germany?

In the beginning of 2004 I received an invitation from Schumacher-Gebler in which he asked me to do a talk on my typeface designs at the TypoTage in Leipzig. Those days I had become a little upset about people asking me about the roots of the DIN typefaces and myself not knowing these, so I decided to speak about their history. I started my investigations at the archive of DIN, i.e. the German Institute of Standardization, in Berlin. In July 2004 I presented my first results at the TypoTage, mainly showing old DIN sheets, funny signposts with DIN typefaces and some comparisons of DIN and FF DIN. One day before my talk a colleague, Martin Binder, told me he had been visiting DIN as well. He had been talking to people which already had retired before 2004 and he kindly gave me some of his photocopies showing the evidence of the involvement of the Siemens engineer Ludwig Goller in the development of DIN 1451 which I then included in my talk. Indra Kupferschmid pointed me at the similarity between DIN and the typefaces of the Prussian Railways. She knew those because her friend had been collecting information on the history of the railways. The next thing to be done was to find out the truth behind Indra's suggestion, which I found at DIN during the next visit. So my first references clearly pointed at Germany. In

The Typographic Universe visualizes the idea that the core of Latin typefaces with best readability ranges between two kinds of contrasts: expansion (blue layer) and translation (red layer) © 1985 by Gerrit Noordzij

prietary typesetting systems of those days. Character sets had to be extended and in some cases the artwork had to be redrawn because the source material did not always fit with our standards. While working on typefaces that way, Volker Küster (my artistical director in the first year at Scangraphic) made me realize that no matter how strange a typeface design might look at first sight, it has its very own integrity. Here I learned that my job was not about finding mistakes and improve on badly drawn curves, it had also become my task to keep the original spirit of the design along that way. URW went through hard times in the years I worked there.

the process I kept finding facts which proved that other versions of the DIN typefaces also clearly origin in models that had been developed by German draughtsmen, engineers and teachers. Next to this I discovered that they could have been influenced by developments in other countries. From a historical point of view though, it is sometimes hard to find evidence that truly proves who influenced who and to what extend, but I think that I can say that in the 19th century the Germans had established quite an autonomous tradition of drawing sans serifs by means of construction schemes.

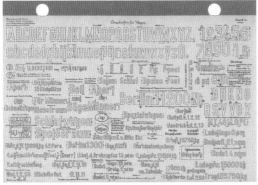

Masterdrawing IV 44 4th Edition from 1912 by the "Königliche Preussische Eisenbahn", the Royal Prussian Railways. The letterforms are identical with the first version from 1905. This typeface is known as the official model for DIN Engschrift which was developed between 1926 and 1936.

When type designers talk about FF DIN they are impressed by the improvements you did to DIN 1451 without imposing your personality over the aesthetics of the original. Having such a well-known brand as DIN 1451, was it hard to design FF DIN without losing the "taste" of the original?

First of all, the DIN typefaces were only known and used amongst a few pioneering designers before FSI released FF DIN. The design community was either not aware of their existence, or they thought that they were rubbish. Until the late eighties, most leading designers propagated sans serifs such as Univers, Hel-

vetica, Futura or Akzidenz Grotesk. Eventually they would also name Gill or Syntax, but those days even these typefaces were considered as slightly exotic. After having taken a closer look at DIN, I figured that there were basically two ways of reviving it. Sure it can be interesting to enhance some of the peculiarities of a typeface to make it look funny and trendy. Considering that DIN had been developed with the aim to make it look "normal" that would not do justice to the name of the typeface. Also a user does not expect a typeface to be funny when its name relates to things such as norms.

Modern Sans Serifs (expansion)

Hamburgefonts

Helvetica (1957)

Hamburgefonts

Univers (1957)

Hamburgefonts

FF DIN (1995)

Humanist Sans Serifs (translation)

Hamburgefonts

Gill Sans (1928)

Hamburgefonts

Syntax (1968)

Hamburgefonts

Frutiger (1976)

Many modernist designers have been propagating the exclusive use of the select choice of modern sans serif typefaces shown above. Frutiger was the first humanist sans they gradually accepted.

In 1995 FontShop International published FF DIN as a FontFont. This book is the best proof that the typeface has been very successful ever since and keeps on being very attractive for designers. Why do you think FF DIN became that successful?

In September 2001 my late friend and type designer Evert Bloemsma and I attended ATypI Copenhagen. On the ferry from Denmark to Germany he took a small piece of paper on which he wrote:

"80% high-tech, coolness, 10% charming imperfection, 10% mechanical look-and-feel."

With his typical intrigued look he told me these were the three reasons why FF DIN had become so successful. Concerning "high-tech and coolness" I think that this was welcomed as an opposite to the post-modernist trends we have seen going by. Apart from that, our media tend to become crowded with things that used to be too expensive and/or too complex such as images and full-color in printed objects as well as animated graphics and movies in websites. Thus it appears logical that designers have been looking for counterparts to those. Typefaces like FF DIN exactly fulfil this demand and help the designer to create spaces where readers can sort of chill out and concentrate on the message behind all the fireworks. Just as Erik Spiekermann, author of "Stop Stealing Sheep" wrote in his book, DIN is the magic word for everything that can be measured in Germany and that designers like DIN's lean geometric lines, features that don't make it the best choice for signage. Evert's remarks about the charming imperfection and the mechanical look show that I have probably been successful in maintaining the spirit of the original character of DIN.

In my own opinion, FF DIN's success is equally based on three things:

—The abbreviation DIN is something which many designers easily make associations with. Starting with obvious ones like (German) industrial quality and maintaining standards, one can easily imagine that DIN is also being associated with things such as being accurate, striving for the perfect, and most of all: neutrality.

—FontShop's marketing power: Most graphic designers have experienced this along their projects. No matter how well the design of your magazine, campaign, packaging or website may be, it needs a good concept and a lot of marketing power to make sure that you get the attention needed. When it comes to typefaces this is often not fully understood. Yes, it is relatively easy to offer your typeface through some online-shop, but that is only the very first step. Typeface designs are products which have the potential to be used all over the world. Well known typeface designs usually outlive global corporate design projects by decades, so in order to compete in the long run, on a global scale and keep in sync with technical developments you need a structure that is able to guarantee the technical and artistical maintenance needed to ensure that they can last on the market for ages.

—The fact that I mainly improved the overall quality of the design and extended the typeface family whilst respecting the look and feel of the intentions it was made with. On Typophile Erik recently has put it this way: "FF DIN looks as if DIN had always had those weights because Albert didn't let his ego interfere with the job." This is one of the biggest compliments I ever had!

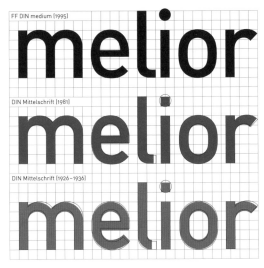

FF DIN medium (1995)

DIN Mittelschrift (1981)

DIN Mittelschrift (1926–1936)

Comparison of FF DIN (top and outlines) and DIN from 1981 (middle) resp. 1936 (bottom). In this illustration, the spacing of FF DIN and DIN from 1981 has been adjusted to match the spacing of DIN from 1936. For FF DIN, the grid and the single stroke weight were abandoned. The weight of the horizontal curves has been reduced. Curves, and their transitions into straight lines were designed fluently. Speaking in terms of the Typographic Universe, the subtle modifications in stroke weight enabled the typeface to move into the lowest line of the blue expansion layer. DIN Mittelschrift is doomed to stay outside the Universe because its horizontal and vertical strokes have exactly the same weight.

strous octopus which tries to catch your attention by providing many arms that are styled in every variation you might think of. From a logical point of view it seems the right thing to do, but from a marketing point of view we must also consider that a typeface family must still be recognizable as such. When family members become so extravagant that they are not being recognized as such anymore, the family will loose its integrity and become an endangered species. Speaking in terms of the Typographic Universe one might say that this is often the case with typeface families whose members live in layers with different colors. Especially Rotis and also Compatil are examples of such families. Still we have some variations "under construction" which are quite unusual for a sans serif typeface family, so there are some things to look out for!

round	**FF DIN**		italic	condensed	cond. italic
ая	аяε	*light*	*ая*	*ая*	*ая*
ая	аяε	*regular*	*ая*	*ая*	*ая*
ая	аяε	*medium*	*ая*	*ая*	*ая*
ая	аяε	*bold*	*ая*	*ая*	*ая*
ая	аяε	*black*	*ая*	*ая*	*ая*

latin cyrillic greek

FF DIN and FF DIN Round family overview

FF DIN has turned into a super family. There are five weights of FF DIN, FF DIN Condensed and FF DIN Round, as well as Greek and Cyrillic versions. Are there any plans to let the family even grow more?

Of course we are working on new extensions and have made plans for others. On the other hand, it does not make sense to just add what seems to be possible. Doing so we could make almost any typeface-family look like a mon-

Thank you for your time!

R

Matt Adams' Favorite
DIN Letter is "R".

Brighton
2009 – Poster, Newspaper
Design Matt Adams

"Brighton" is a self-initiated
documentation of a two week
period within the town. A single
color, overprinted newspaper,
and A2 posters were created as
a response.

BRIGHTON
—
A documentation of Brighton over a two week
period, in Easter, of two thousand and nine.
—
Thirty slash four slash nine
to ten slash four slash nine.

30/04/09
to 10/04/09

"*For its clean aesthetic and ability to portray information in the most legible way.*"

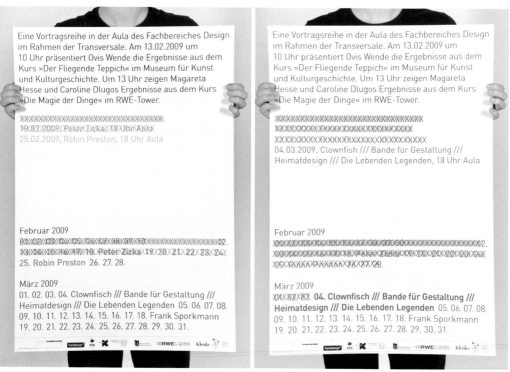

Transversale
2009 – Poster
Client Transversale
Design Marvin Boiko

The screen-printed poster follows a strict rule: The actual events are shown colored while older events are crossed out. The calendar contains the upcoming events of the symposium.

0

"The information on the poster changes after a few days. I needed a font that provides the possibility to be overprinted by itself without becoming unreadable. You can hide the DIN light underneath the bold weight because of its symmetrical dimensions. The DIN was the perfect font for this project."

Marvin Boiko's
Favorite DIN Letter
is "O".

Eine Vortragsreihe in der Aula des Fachbereiches Design
im Rahmen der Transversale. Am 13.02.2009 um
10 Uhr präsentiert Ovis Wende die Ergebnisse aus dem
Kurs »Der Fliegende Teppich« im Museum für Kunst
und Kulturgeschichte. Um 13 Uhr zeigen Magareta
Hesse und Caroline Dlugos Ergebnisse aus dem Kurs
»Die Magie der Dinge« im RWE-Tower.

XXXXXXXXXXXXXXXXXXXXXXXXXXXXX
XXXXXXXXXXXXXXXXXXXXXXXXXXXXX
XXXXXXXXXXXXXXXXXXXXXXXXXXXXX
04.03.2009, Clownfisch /// Bande für Gestaltung ///
Heimatdesign /// Die Lebenden Legenden, 18 Uhr Aula
18.03.2009, Frank Sporkmann, 18 Uhr Aula

Februar 2009
XXXXXXXXXXXXXXXXXXXXXXXXXXXXXXXXXXXXXXXX 2.
XXXXXXXXXXXXXXX Peter Zizka /// 20. 21. 22. 23. 24.
XXXXXXXXXXXXXXXX 26. 27. 28.

März 2009
01. 02. 03. 04. Clownfisch /// Bande für Gestaltung ///
Heimatdesign /// Die Lebenden Legenden 05. 06. 07. 08.
09. 10. 11. 12. 13. 14. 15. 16. 17. 18. Frank Sporkmann
19. 20. 21. 22. 23. 24. 25. 26. 27. 28. 29. 30. 31.

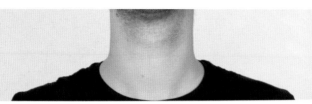

Eine Vortragsreihe in der Aula des Fachbereiches Design
im Rahmen der Transversale. Am 13.02.2009 um
10 Uhr präsentiert Ovis Wende die Ergebnisse aus dem
Kurs »Der Fliegende Teppich« im Museum für Kunst
und Kulturgeschichte. Um 13 Uhr zeigen Magareta
Hesse und Caroline Dlugos Ergebnisse aus dem Kurs
»Die Magie der Dinge« im RWE-Tower.

11.02.2009, Daniele Buetti, 16 Uhr Aula

Februar 2009
01. 02. 03. 04. 05. 06. 07. 08. 09. 10. 11. Daniele Buetti 12.
13. 14. 15. 16. 17. 18. Peter Zizka 19. 20. 21. 22. 23. 24.
25. Robin Preston 26. 27. 28.

März 2009
01. 02. 03. 04. Clownfisch /// Bande für Gestaltung ///
Heimatdesign /// Die Lebenden Legenden 05. 06. 07. 08.
09. 10. 11. 12. 13. 14. 15. 16. 17. 18. Frank Sporkmann
19. 20. 21. 22. 23. 24. 25. 26. 27. 28. 29. 30. 31.

Eine Vortragsreihe in der Aula des Fachbereiches Design
im Rahmen der Transversale. Am 13.02.2009 um
10 Uhr präsentiert Ovis Wende die Ergebnisse aus dem
Kurs »Der Fliegende Teppich« im Museum für Kunst
und Kulturgeschichte. Um 13 Uhr zeigen Magareta
Hesse und Caroline Dlugos Ergebnisse aus dem Kurs
»Die Magie der Dinge« im RWE-Tower.

XXXXXXXXXXXXXXXXXXXXXXXXXXXXXXXXX
18.02.2009, Peter Zizka, 18 Uhr Aula

Februar 2009
01. 02. 03. 04. 05. 06. 07. 08. 09. 10. XXXXXXXXXXXXXXXXXXXXXXXX12.
13. 14. 15. 16. 17. **18. Peter Zizka** 19. 20. 21. 22. 23. 24.
25. Robin Preston 26. 27. 28.

März 2009
01. 02. 03. 04. Clownfisch /// Bande für Gestaltung ///
Heimatdesign /// Die Lebenden Legenden 05. 06. 07. 08.
09. 10. 11. 12. 13. 14. 15. 16. 17. 18. Frank Sporkmann
19. 20. 21. 22. 23. 24. 25. 26. 27. 28. 29. 30. 31.

**Between Land
and Sea**
2008 – Poster,
Invitation
Client International
Center for Fine Art
Research
Design Paulus M.
Dreibholz

The show was about four UK-based artists presenting work at a Belgian gallery Box33. Inspired by this theme, the poster-side of the product, featuring the title of the show, has been treated like a maritime map displaying the passage between Belgium and the UK that has to be passed through if one travels by boat from one country to the other. Since the work shown in the exhibition was of a very contemporary nature, we wanted the product to reflect this aspect in its design.

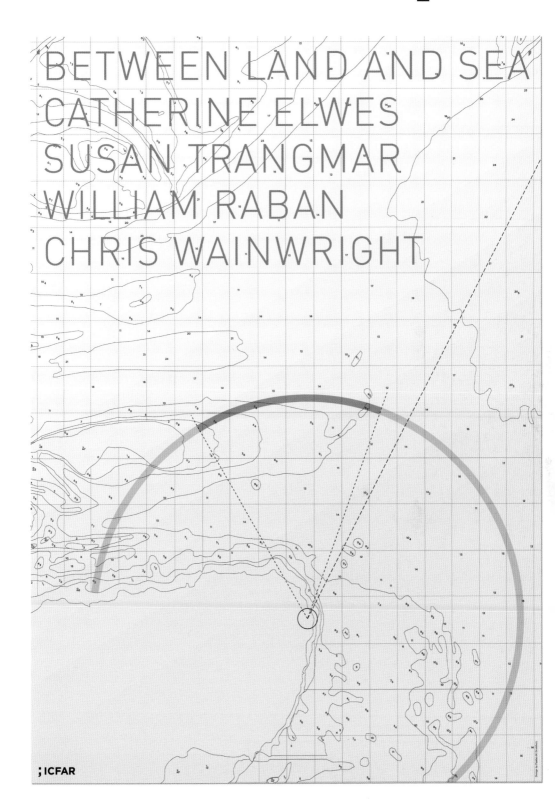

BETWEEN LAND AND SEA
CATHERINE ELWES
SUSAN TRANGMAR
WILLIAM RABAN
CHRIS WAINWRIGHT

; ICFAR

3

Paulus M. Dreibholz's
Favorite DIN Number
is "3".

"DIN, being a very engineered type, with little fancy and pragmatic in nature, lent itself beautifully to complete the task we set out to pursue. The light version of the type shown in 100% cyan integrated perfectly well with the neatly printed lines in grey while the small numbers indicating depth remained legible at the very small sizes they were used."

Full Color Version

Black & White Version

Ken Lo's Favorite DIN
Letter is "G".

Backroom Conversations
2010 – Corporate Identity
Client Asia Art Archive
Design Blow (Ken Lo)

Backroom Conversations includes panel discussions and
screenings that touch on a number of prevalent issues and
offer a first-hand look into today's world of contemporary
art. This is about exploring the scene behind art. I was
asked to design the VI and collaterals for the event.

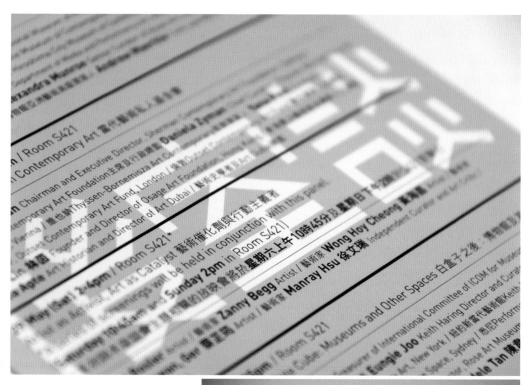

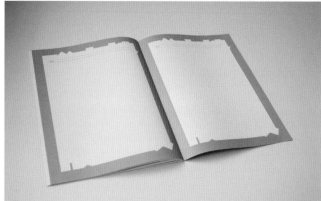

*"The typeface DIN gives
the project a modern
touch."*

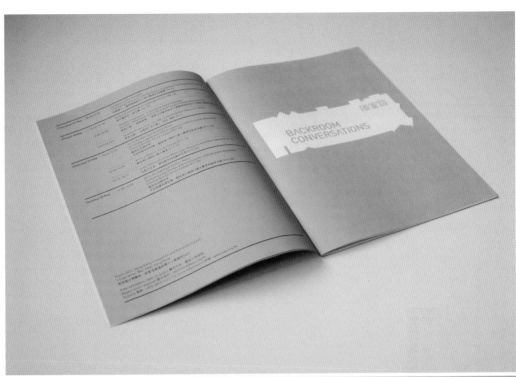

R

Cypher13's Favorite
DIN Letter is "R".

"DIN Next was chosen for its rich history and heritage in delivering information specific to the fields of engineering, technology, and business. This connection was particularly poignant as the three are key components to the inaugural Biennial of the Americas. When producing an international identity, legibility is always a concern and Kobayashi's updated DIN Next is second to none."

Biennial of the Americas
2010 – Identity, Exhibition Graphics,
Collateral, Program
Client Biennial of the Americas
Design Cypher13

The Biennial of the Americas identity is a tribute to the Americas as a diverse and intimately connected hemispheric community. The inherent vascularity of the Logomark represents the free exchange and continual flow of culturally-inspired innovation between North, Central, and South America. The various segments of the Logomark and corresponding colors represent the four interconnected Biennial themes. Blue communicates truth and innovation, green represents the quest for heightened sustainability, brown stands for earth and the Americas community, and orange represents the arts and the wisdom gained through collaboration. The soft and subtle curvature of the mark emphasizes the organic evolution of the Americas as a collective - one hemisphere united.

To communicate the wide array of Biennial programming occurring within the McNichol's Building at Civic Center Park, a printed program was designed and produced. The Nature of Things program's cover was printed in the four colors of the Biennial, representing community, art, innovation, and sustainability. Careful attention was paid to information organization to maximize space and to minimize resources.

Typeface in Use
DIN, Hiragino Gothic
[Japanese character]

"Because DIN is polished and simple."

Tohoku Rakuten Golden Eagles
2009 – Season Tickets Book and
Box
Client Rakuten Yakyudan
Art Direction Commune (Ryo Ueda)
Design Commune (Ryo Ueda,
Minami Mabuchi)
Planning Shinji Yoshikawa, Tomoki
Negishi

The theme of creation for us is to
make something better. Inspired by
the will to make something better,
our design work may move people
or make society work a little better.
It's like giving a gift. We choose a
gift with the idea of delighting that
special someone. It's a pleasure
for us to be able to present something the recipient does not expect

and truly appreciates. At times, our creations take people
by surprise, awake their emotions, or even move them to
tears. That's exactly what we're looking for to create.

"DIN's confident, rational and highly distinctive characteristics perfectly complement the values of The Nth Degree Club. The typeface's combination of both classical and contemporary qualities make it a perfect fit for a brand that re-imagines the traditional members' club for savvy, discerning consumers."

Typeface in Use
DIN

R

Ragged Edge Design's
Favorite DIN Letter
is "R".

The Nth Degree Club
2010 – Corporate Identity
Client The Nth Degree Club
Design Ragged Edge Design (Max Ottignon, Luke Woodhouse)

The Nth Degree Club is an online members' club offering access to world-class events, money can't buy opportunities and networking events.

The visual identity, created by Ragged Edge Design, communicates the brand's re-imagining of the private members' club concept by combining classical sensibilities with a contemporary aesthetic.

The identity centres around a bold, confident "N" marque that can be used with or without the accompanying logotype. Instantly recognizable and authoritative, it is designed to add a layer of mystery and exclusivity to the brand's covetable offer.

S

Mortar&Pestle's
Favorite DIN Letter
is "S".

My Personal Assistant
2010 – Corporate
Identity
Client My Personal
Assistant
Design Mortar&Pestle
Studio

Client is a London-based service company
which operates to provide secretary services for business and at a personal level. To
highlight their particular business aspect in
the identity, we started off by incorporating
imagery of personal agenda into their stationery, promotional materials and website design.
We drilled 5 mm holes along the margin of
everything they printed which could be filled
into a ring binder folder. Using DIN we felt that
we would achieve a look that best represented
themselves.

"We felt that the typeface DIN, lent itself to certain organizational qualities and this would help communicate what the client does. They are personal assistants for external businesses and this is how they wanted to be seen by their clients."

Typeface in Use
DIN Regular, DIN Light, DIN Bold

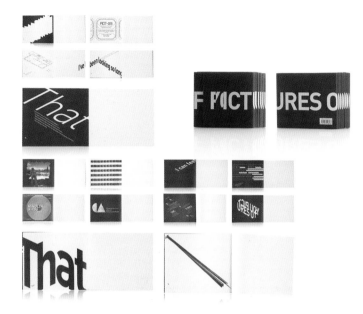

Typeface in Use
DIN

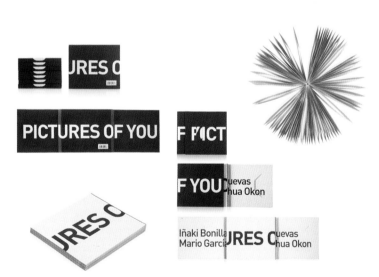

Menosunocerouno's
Favorite DIN Letter
is "A".

"We used DIN for this project because it is a very clean type. DIN, as a neutral typeface; can be used for many different purposes. One of the most important assets it has is the multiple weights of the family. The combination of this features, made DIN the right choice for this specific task."

Pictures Of You
2002 – Art Catalog
Client Americas Society
Design Menosunocerouno

Menosunocerouno was commissioned to design a publication for the art exhibition Pictures Of You at The Americas Society Art Gallery in New York City. The exhibition featured young mexican artists Iñaki Bonillas, Mario García Torres, Minerva Cuevas and Joshua Okon, curated by Sofía Hernandez Chong Cuy. The book was designed with a very tight printing budget in mind.

The result was a publication using papel revolución that is usually used to wrap tortillas and be bound as notepads, and packed in a box for protection. Pictures Of You was distributed during the exhibition at the gallery. The inspiration for the exhibition title and the book was the song Pictures Of You performed by The Cure in the 1990s.

Big Room
2009 – Corporate Identity, Stationery
Client Big Room Pty Ltd.
Design Glasfurd & Walker (Phoebe Glasfurd)

The project was about creating an identity and
branding strategies for a company that advo-
cates environmentally friendly practices with
unconventional views and approaches. The
goal is to give the company a face that merges
the idea of the client being both a corporate
and an environmental group while shunning
the stereotypical "green" connotations in the
design.

**Glasfurd & Walker's
Favorite DIN Letter
is "O".**

<u>Typeface in Use</u>
DIN Light, DIN Regular

*"Complimented the monogram with
a clean, modern and professional
aesthetic that was less traditional
than other corporate companies in
their niche."*

The Most Honest
2009 – Packaging
Client Chocolat Factory
Creative Direction Ruiz+Company (David Ruiz)
Design Ruiz+Company (Vicente Ruiz)

The first chocolate bar that defies honesty, specifying
the exact number of calories per serving, in an austerely
designed and informative package typical of the brand,
where the chocolate takes centre stage.

"(DIN) was used as a corporative typeface for the
brand Chocolat Factory. We used this typeface
because it is simple, plain, sans serif and has
a lot of character and temperament."

The Souvenirs
2009 – Packaging
Client Chocolat Factory
Creative Direction Ruiz+Company
(David Ruiz)
Art Direction Ruiz+Company
(Ainhoa Nagore)
Design Ruiz+Company
(Vicente Ruiz)
Copy Jorge Alavedra

Line of packs designed for Chocolat Factory and sold in the airports
of the main Spanish cities. With
a postcard/box and a slogan à la
James Bond, we make chocolates
the best "made in Spain" souvenir.

5

Ruiz+Company's
Favorite DIN Number
is "5".

Bars
2008 – Packaging
Client Chocolat Factory
Creative Direction Ruiz+Company (David Ruiz)
Design Ruiz+Company
Copy María Ruiz

Chocolat Factory, bars. Following the brand identity's
graphic criterion, austere luxury, the new line of bars has
been created using a color coding that relates to the type
of cocoa used for each bar, while the writing provides only
the information that's absolutely relevant, such as the type
of cocoa or where it comes from. Forcefulness, differentia-
tion and brand personality.

Ellg Gourmet
2008 – Packaging
Client ELLG Gourmet
Design thisislove studio
(Joana Areal)
Photography Paulo Andrade

Ellg Gourmet chocolate seduces who tries it,
distinguishes who offers it.

Identity, packaging and online-store for the
gourmet chocolate brand "with a twist".

Ellg Gourmet stands for full creativity asso-
ciating "converted cocoa" – chocolate - with
several ingredients and spices to result in surprising combinations and different flavours.

The pastel colors differentiate and identify all
handmade chocolates, truffles, cookies and
other delights made by Ellg Gourmet.

*"For its delicate yet
strong structure."*

C

thisislove studio's
Favorite DIN Letter
is "C".

Typeface in Use
DIN

"The bulky and con-structed aspect of DIN matches the feeling of industrial construction which characterize shipping containers."

London, 08/09/08

Edgar Wallace
Transatlantic Shipping Co.
37, Green Court
Manchester

Concerning: Shipping container for Shanghai

Dear Mr. Wallace,

One morning, when Gregor Samsa woke from troubled dreams, he found himself transformed in his bed into a horrible vermin. He lay on his armour-like back, and if he lifted his head a little he could see his brown belly, slightly domed and divided by arches into stiff sections. The bedding was hardly able to cover it and seemed ready to slide off any moment.

His many legs, pitifully thin compared with the size of the rest of him, waved about helplessly as he looked. "What's happened to me?" he thought. It wasn't a dream. His room, a proper human room although a little too small, lay peacefully between its four familiar walls. A collection of textile samples lay spread out on the table - Samsa was a travelling salesman and above it there hung a picture that he had recently cut out of an illustrated magazine and housed in a nice, gilded frame.

Best regards,

Jonas Wandeler's Favorite DIN Letter is "P".

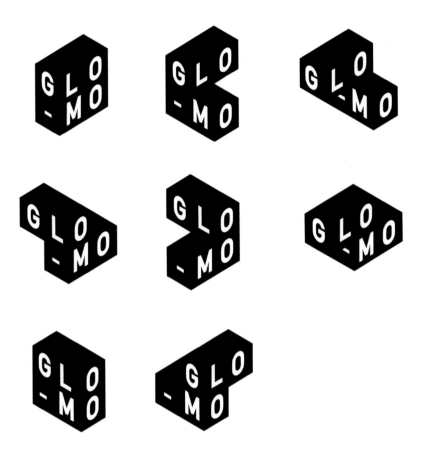

Glomo
2008 – Corporate Identity
Client Global Modular Company
Design Jonas Wandeler for Graphic Thought Facility

Modular logo for Glomo (global modular hotel company), a
British company which builds modular hotels with shipping
containers. The logo reflects the different forms the buildings can take.

Typeface in Use
DIN Bold, DIN Regular, DIN Light

The British Music Experience
2010 – Collateral
Design Lucy Gibson

A project to promote the British music experience exhibition to the British public of all ages. An exhibition that showcased the top ten British iconic artists from the past 30 years. A special edition EP with accompanying biography booklet for each artist and an A2 poster. For the photo shoot, I made photocopies and cut-outs of the featuring artists and sprinkled some red and blue strips all over the images as a vivid montage. It was great fun to shoot and the aesthetic was very pleasing.

21.24 Studio's Favorite
DIN Letter is "t".

Lema
2010 – Press Kit (Bag, Poster and DVD)
Client Lema
Design 21.24 Studio (Simona Frigerio, Paola Castelli)
Photography Ferruccio Zanvettor for Gate8

Introducing new Lema products in occasion of Salone Internazionale
del Mobile di Milano 2010.

*"DIN is our favorite font:
clean and beautiful."*

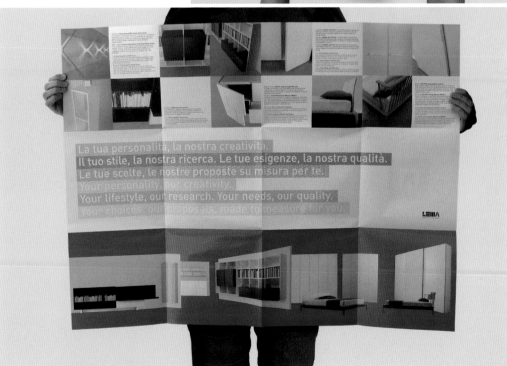

Typeface in Use
DIN Medium, Univers 57 Condensed

LETTING THE CAT OUT OF THE BAG IS A WHOLE LOT EASIER THAN PUTTING IT BACK IN.

O

Martin Asbjørnsen's
Favorite DIN Letter
is "O".

Letting the cat out of the bag...
2010 – Tote Bag Print
Design martinmartin (Martin Asbjørnsen)

Tote bags made for self promotion.

<u>Typeface in Use</u>
DIN 1451 Engschrift

I WAS WALKING ALONG THIS NARROW MOUNTAIN PASS – SO NARROW THAT NOBODY ELSE COULD PASS YOU, WHEN I SAW A BEAUTIFUL BLONDE WALKING TOWARDS ME. **A BEAUTIFUL BLONDE, WITH NOT A STITCH ON** – YES, NOT A STITCH ON LADY, COR BLIMEY. **I DIDN'T KNOW WHETHER TO TOSS MYSELF OFF OR BLOCK HER PASSAGE.**

MAX MILLER

Funny Ha ha
2007 – Book
Client Tokyo Type Director's Club
Design Why Not Associates

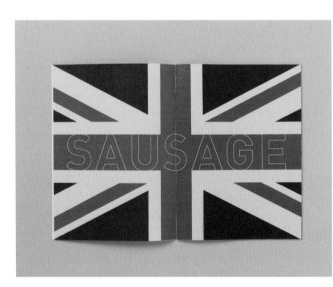

To mark its 20th anniversary, the Tokyo Type Director's Club commissioned and published a series of 20 books, each by a different graphic designer on his or her personally selected theme.

Andy Altmann of Why Not Associates designed a book paying homage to his heroes of British comedy. Jokes were typeset and combined with found photographs of British scenes.

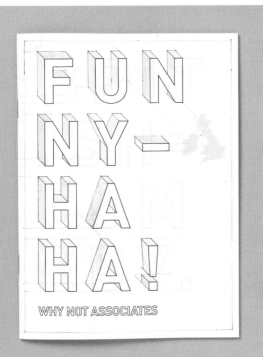

H

Why Not Associates'
Favorite DIN Letter
is "H".

S

SuperBruut's Favorite
DIN Letter is "S".

Typeface in Use
Customized typeface
based upon DIN Eng-
schrift Std

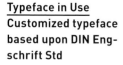

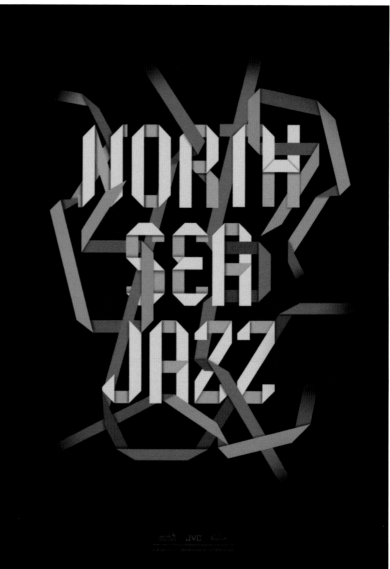

North Sea Jazz Art Poster '10
2010 – Poster
Client North Sea Jazz Festival Art Poster contest
Design SuperBruut (Thijs Janssen)

A text experiment where I used the DIN typeface as
a master for the paper folding simulation. The use of
straight "hard" typo and the lines with the random
bends creates a spontaneous image.

"I like the DIN character forms"

B

Marvin Boiko's
Favorite DIN Letter
is "B".

*"The DIN Mittelschrift
is used within the cor-
porate design of the
University of Applied
Sciences and Arts
Dortmund."*

Buchwoche
2009 – Poster
Client "Fasta Design" (Student council of the University of Applied
Sciences and Arts Dortmund, Germany)
Design Eva Thiessies, Marvin Boiko
Photography Yoko Dupuis

The poster announced a week of exhibitions, lectures and workshops
which took place in 2009 and broached the issue of "books". A capital
letter "B" took its shape as the chopped books and color paper were
put into place.

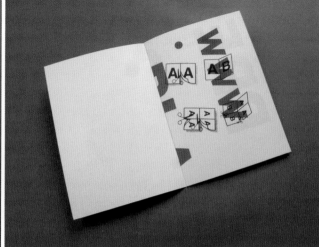

Typeface in Use
DIN Black Alternate

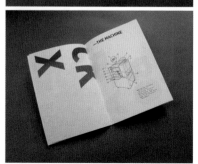

C

Birch Studio Ltd.'s
Favorite DIN Letter
is "C".

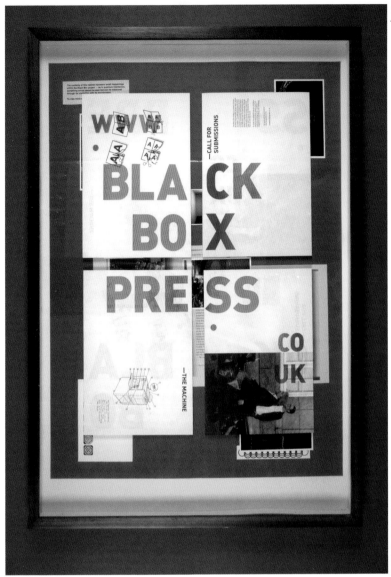

"Bold, clean and functional. DIN is the perfectly functional typeface that could give our message an impact.

Black Box Press
2009 – Sample Book
Client Black Box Press
Design Birch Studio Ltd.

Black Box Press is a non-profit project which helps artists, designers and writers to publish their work. Originally only producing books with a two colour Risograph (including this booklet), DIN reflects the social and functional nature of the press.

The idea behind the booklet was to design something which is versatile and easy to reproduce. It is intended to be send without an envelope using the guides on the back cover and once the booklet has been read it can be used to make a poster.

2

Company's Favorite
DIN Number is "2".

Remap Arts Programme
2010 – Visual identity
Client Remap KM
Design Company (Alex Swain, Chrysostomos
Naselos)

The multi-faceted identity of this vibrant
neighborhood was our inspiration. Striking
images of the various venues were overlaid
with artists' photographs cut out into a shape
that mirrors a map of the area.

These visually arresting images were contrasted with clean typography and graphics
for all information.

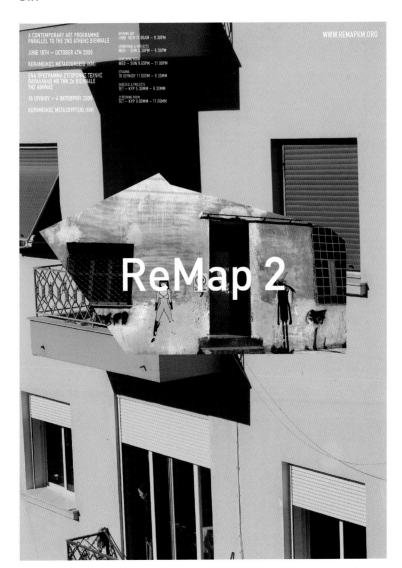

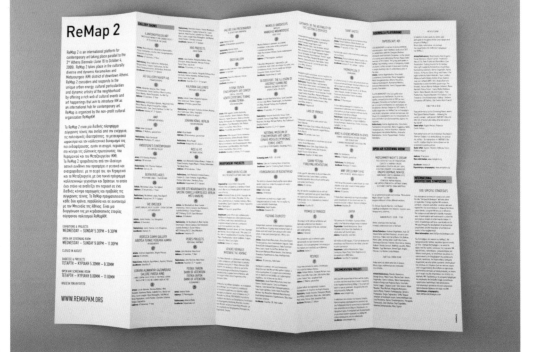

"We chose DIN because of its history, being used for traffic and information signage. It is solid and confident, and also available in Greek and English which was essential for the Remap project."

This poster is for the annual exhibition of the best architecture final projects in 2010 at EPFL.

ARCHIZOOM
2007-2010 – Poster
Client Archizoom
Design Atelier Poisson
(Giorgio Pesce)

Archizoom is the architecture gallery of the Federal Polytechnical School of Lausanne (EPFL). When this gallery decided to change its image, the brief was to make a dramatic change from the usual sober "architecture" style. The first new exhibition was on historical extravagant Italian 70s ARCHIZOOM Group. So I suggested to use it as the name of the new space. And I decided to use a transformed DIN typeface as the link between the very different exhibitions through the year, giving a bold and strong image to this space.

This poster was made for the annual exhibition of the best architecture final projects in 2009 at EPFL.

63

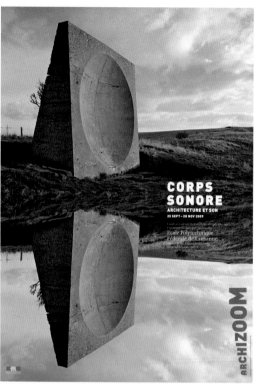

This poster was made for an exhibition of audio/acoustic instal-lations and perform-ances, related to archi-tecture.

Atelier Poisson's Favorite DIN Letter is "O".

Typeface in Use
Customized typeface based upon DIN

This poster was made for an exhibition of an important figure of Swiss architecture, a former teacher at EPFL.

"We developed the logo and all the identity for this architecture gallery based on DIN typeface, redesigned with a 'fat' style to make it particu-lar. This main typo, mixed with Esta, gives a bold image somehow different from the usual 'archi-tecture' renderings."

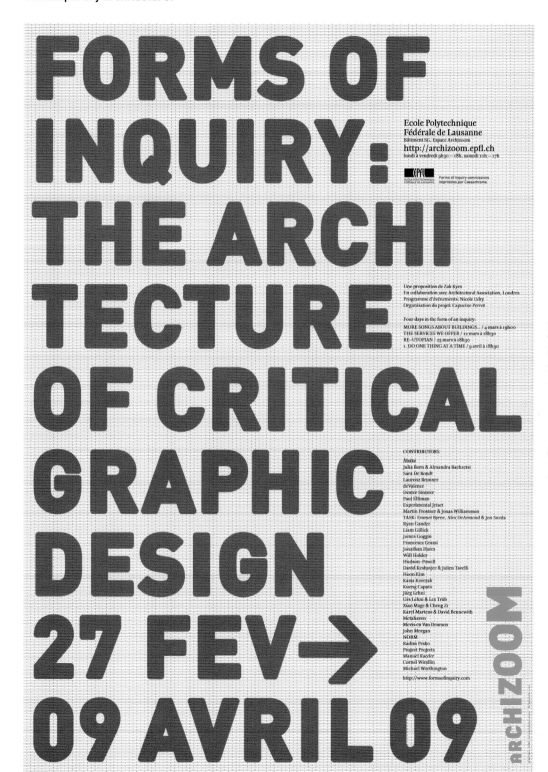

1i

1₂

PAVE MENT

GORI LLAZ

"The reason I used this typeface on this project is because it represents modernism now-adays and something 'tech' that I would like to show. I also used it because of its weight variety and because it is a typeface that can be easily transformed (lettering). And finally I used it because of it's great readability."

Tilt.Festival.Athens
2010 – Corporate Identity, Poster, Merchandise, Signage
Design George Strouzas

The hardest task when developing the branding of the festival was that I had to decide how to place the logo. It had to be on every application but it shouldn't brainwash the viewer. The goal is to make people understand that what they see is part of the festivals experience and not an individual element.

I also learned that intense color contrast can highlight a branding but it must be supported differently every time using typography, illustration and photography. For all the applications that I designed, I used grid systems (different every time); this helped me to control the white space and make the layouts look very solid.

The whole emphasis of the branding of the
music festival is based on typography; I used
PF Din Text Pro in various sizes and styles.
Apparently in some applications, like the logo,
I used the forms of the letters based on PF Din
Text Pro but I redesigned all the letters, so
it is a combo of a typeface and custom -made
lettering where the goal is to have unique
style and aesthetics.

While designing with typography and without
using unnecessary stuff that would make the
work look amateur, I came to realize that it
is hard to show intensity with so few things.
When I found out that I could manage to show
additional information taken from the spon-
sors it was critical, since they helped me
to solve lots of problems and gave me the
amount of info I needed each time helping
me to define a style to the whole branding.
The lettering with its unique style makes this
project a live experiment, because every time
I had to design a word I also had to make it
look great and legible but not brighter than
the logo.

R

George Strouzas'
Favorite DIN Letter
is "R".

T ZIJ TOT HAAR
RVAREN DAT
RIJWEL GEHEEL
L VAN HET
VEEN

ERLIJKRECHT — J.B. SPATH
KINDERTAXI))

DAARBIJ HEEFT
ONTZETTING ER
HAAR HAND VR
IN DE SCHEDEL
MEISJE VERDW

JURISPRUDENTIE — BURGE
(HR 22-02-02, NJ 2002 (KI

RLIJKRECHT — J.B. SPATH
NDERTAXI))

JURISPRUDENTIE — BURG
(HR 22-02-02, NJ 2002 (K

XIBUS REED
N VAN DE
WIELEN
AAR HOOFD.

DEZE TAXIBU
MET EEN VA
ACHTERWIEL
OVER HAAR

"The use of the clean
and universal form of
the typeface is good
for giving information.
And the typeface won't
bring a lot of 'feeling'
with it."

HIJ DRINKT
MEER EN IS
TROTS LID V
ANONIEME A

E RAINMAKER — IS A 1995
VEL BY JOHN GRISHAM.

THE RAINMAKER — IS A 1
NOVEL BY JOHN GRISHAM

Typeface in Use
DIN Engschrift Std

VREDE VAN DE HEER

IN DE VRED

1ONE SIMONE

R VAN MEVROUW VERA SIMONE EN HEER BERT SIMONE

IL 2009

SIMON

DOCHTER VAN MI

9 APRIL 200

9 april jongslede is
lochter van v. Simone
toen vijf jaar oud was,
en verkeersongeval
het leven gekomen."

"Op 9 ap
de doch
die toen
bij een
om het

ER GEVE HAAR ZIEL DE EEUWIGE RUST

ENTIE – BURGERLIJKRECHT – J.B. SPATH : (HR 22-02-02, NJ 2002 (KINDERTAXI))

DE HEER GI

JURISPRUDENTIE – BUI

Plagiarism Story
2009 – Poster
Design SuperBruut
(Thijs Janssen)

The series of posters of a story consists sentences from different sources which together form a new story. The story can be divided into five parts. 1. There is nothing wrong (happy), 2. The accident, 3. Child dies, 4. Official death (funeral) and 5. Grieving. I've tried to capture these events in five posters. A small English summary about the story: The story is about a man in a van, who runs over a little girl with the rear tire. The little girl dies instantly. The man behind the wheel goes behind bars for twenty-seven years (based on a true story).

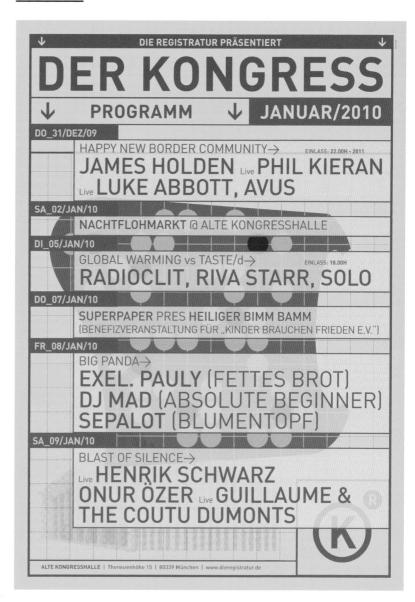

Der Kongress
2009 – Corporate
Identity, Poster,
Advertising Material
Client Der Kongress
Design designliga
(Andreas Döhring)

Der Kongress is a platform for wide-ranging activities including DJ sets, parties, exhibitions, readings and workshops. Der Kongress is the interface of a diverse range of activities, a hub of the city's subculture where the free flow of ideas and thoughts in Munich comes together for a moment. Events are held in varying locations and in the Congress Hall of Munich's former exhibition centre. Der Kongress was the successor of Die Registratur.

The logo is a subtly designed advancement of the logo of Die Registratur to generate the desired brand recognition. Screen design is kept uncluttered, discreet and clear to focus attention on the various platforms.

Typeface in Use
FF DIN

DIE REGISTRATUR PRÄSENTIERT

OKT/NOV

↓ PROGRAMM ↓

FR_09/OKT/09 — EINLASS: 23.00 UHR

ALTE KONGRESSHALLE→
BOYS NOIZE POWER WORLD TOUR
BOYSNOIZE, DJEDJOTRONIC

SA_10/OKT/09 — EINLASS: 21.30 UHR

ALTE KONGRESSHALLE→
LIVE ON STAGE→ BURAKA SOM SISTEMA
IM ANSCHLUSS→ YUM YUM MIT CHROME, NOT FX

FR_06/NOV/09 — EINLASS: 23.00 UHR

ALTE KONGRESSHALLE→ 20 JAHRE GROOVE
LIVE PAUL KALKBRENNER, LIVE NÔZE,
MATHIAS AGUAYO, ROLAND APPEL, TELONIUS,
PERM VAC DJ TEAM

SA_07/NOV/09 — EINLASS: 23.00 UHR

ALTE KONGRESSHALLE→ YUM YUM
CHROME, KAMIKAZE, NOT FX

SPECIAL

SA_14/NOV/09
ALTES RATHAUS→ THE GOMMA SUPERSHOW

ALTE KONGRESSHALLE ⓀR

Logo:

ALTE KONGRESSHALLE, Theresienhöhe 17, 80339 München

DIE REGISTRATUR PRÄSENTIERT — DIE REGISTRATUR PRÄSENTIERT

OKTOBER — NOVEMBER

↓ PROGRAMM ↓ — ↓ PROGRAMM ↓

FR_09/OKT/09 — EINLASS: 23.00 UHR

ALTE KONGRESSHALLE→
BOYS NOIZE POWER WORLD TOUR
BOYSNOIZE, DJEDJOTRONIC

SA_10/OKT/09 — EINLASS: 21.30 UHR

ALTE KONGRESSHALLE→
LIVE ON STAGE→ BURAKA SOM SISTEMA

IM ANSCHLUSS→ YUM YUM
MIT CHROME, NOT FX

FR_06/NOV/09 — EINLASS: 23.00 UHR

ALTE KONGRESSHALLE→
20 JAHRE GROOVE
LIVE PAUL KALKBRENNER,
LIVE NÔZE,
MATHIAS AGUAYO, ROLAND APPEL,
TELONIUS, PERM VAC DJ TEAM

SA_07/NOV/09 — EINLASS: 23.00 UHR

ALTE KONGRESSHALLE→ YUM YUM
CHROME, KAMIKAZE, NOT FX

SPECIAL

SA_14/NOV/09
ALTES RATHAUS→
THE GOMMA SUPERSHOW

ALTE KONGRESSHALLE ⓀR

Logo:

ALTE KONGRESSHALLE, Theresienhöhe 17, 80339 München

SP
Sportspark

03 Badminton & Squash

Sometimes size really does matter and that's why we have not one but two of the largest sports halls in the country with 20 Badminton Courts at your disposal. We also have five excellent glass-backed squash courts for your use as well.

See the reverse for more details or ask for a leaflet at Reception.

SP
Sportspark

04 Soccerpark

There are more small sided soccer pitches at Sportspark than anywhere else in East Anglia.

Plus, we are adding three more pitches during the season!

See the reverse for more details or ask for a leaflet at Reception.

SP
Sportspark

05 Aerobics and Dance Classes

With a wide range of classes, daytime or evening, there's always a class to suit you.

Our fantastic air-conditioned studio has a sprung wooden floor and superb views across Eartham Park.

Best of all, there's no need to book – just get your ticket at Reception and join the class.

See the reverse for more details or ask for a leaflet at Reception.

SP
Sportspark

10 Courses

Ever fancied learning a new sport or getting back into sport after an injury? If so, our six week courses with a qualified instructor will help you get started or improve your skills.

A programme for adults and juniors runs throughout the year with one-off taster sessions available.

See the reverse for more details or ask for a leaflet at Reception.

SP
Sportspark

11 Martial Arts

Take a look at our Martial Arts Room which holds classes in a variety of Martial Arts and hosts Table Tennis too.

See the reverse for more details or ask for a leaflet at Reception.

SP
Sportspark

12 Children's Parties

Want to offer your child something memorable or a day with that special touch for their birthday? Sportspark offers exciting and active parties for your child in a fantastic environment.

See the reverse for more details or ask for a leaflet at Reception.

S

The Click Design Consultants' Favorite DIN Letter is "S".

Typeface in Use
DIN

SP
Sportspark

Sportspark Brand Communications
2010 – Brand Identity, Advertising Campaign, Printed Literature
Client Sportspark
Art Direction Bobby Burrage
Design The Click Design Consultants

02 Fitness
With over 80 cardiovascular and weight stack machines plus free weights in our air-conditioned Fitness Centre, we've got all the equipment you'll ever need.
Our Fitness Advisors are all Sports Science graduates which means that you'll get the best advice possible.
See the reverse for more details or ask for a leaflet at Reception.

Sportspark, the largest indoor sports facility in the UK, required a new identity, advertising campaign and printed literature. We chose to launch Sportspark's new identity by featuring it at the heart of a new multi-media advertising campaign, whilst a new range of printed literature showcases the diverse range of activities and sports on offer.

SP
Sportspark

08 Daytime Activities
There's always something for everyone to do during the day at Sportspark. A chance to be active, to learn a new activity in a social setting or to make new friends.
All sessions are led by suitably qualified and experienced instructors who make sure everyone is welcomed.
See the reverse for more details or ask for a leaflet at Reception.

SP
Sportspark

01 Swimming
A world-class pool, offering some of the finest swimming facilities in Britain. Our spotless changing rooms and crystal clear water make the whole experience so much more enjoyable for lane swimmers and fun seekers alike.
Daytime classes include ante-natal, parent & toddler, and adult swimming lessons – see Daytime Activities leaflet.
Lanes are always available for public swimming, apart from galas - see website for updates.
See the reverse for more details or ask for a leaflet at Reception.

"We chose DIN for its simplicity and elegance. We required a typeface, which delivered the message without competing with the imagery or distracting from the information. Furthermore, we considered DIN to have a timeless quality, which was specifically important, given we used it for the identity itself.

G

Neil Wengerd's
Favorite DIN Letter
is "G".

Typeface in Use
DIN Bold,
DIN Medium,
DIN Regular

"DIN's clean lines and timeless feel
paired perfectly with the abstract
mark created for Southwest."

Southwest Airlines Identity
2009 – Corporate Identity, Poster
Design Neil Wengerd

Southwest Airlines is a low-cost carrier based in Texas, with its largest focus on Las Vegas' McCarren International Airport. It is the largest airline in the United States by number of passengers carried, the sixth largest airline by revenue and the fifth largest by fleet size. In spite of the success, their current identity was disjointed. Not all planes shared the same color scheme, and the "updated" planes had only a slight change in color with no change to design. Two to three different logos could also be found in use. A new mark was created based on SWA's historic triangle of airports and representing growth and an expanding catalogue of destinations; a graphic language using linear patterns to represent airline flight traffic tied the identity together visually and conceptually. DIN was chosen as the primary typeface because of the need to create a modern, timeless feeling to evoke the great graphic programs of airlines in the mid-20th century.

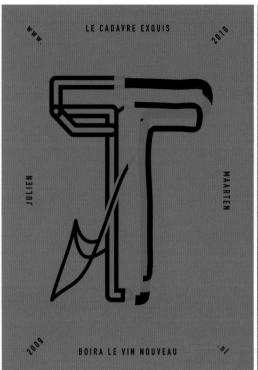
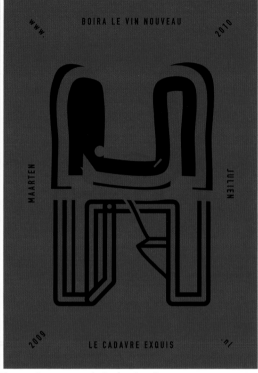

Le cadavre exquis boira le vin nouveau
2010 – Poster
Design Julien Arts, Maarten van Gent

C - Curious, A - Act, D - DADA, A- Answer,
V - Visual, R - React, E - Experiment/ Exchange,
X - Xeno, Q - Quest, U - Us, I - Infinity,
S - Surprising

"We needed a typeface with a clear outline/shape to doodle on. The DIN gives a simple but distinct feeling which gave the final piece a nice starting point."

MAARTEN

WWW.

2010

BOIRA LE VIN NOUVEAU

LE CADAVRE EXQUIS

2009

JULIEN

.lu

S

Thijs Janssen's
Favorite DIN Letter
is "S".

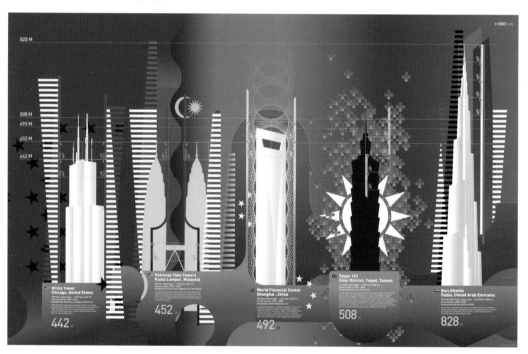

*"The use of the clean
and universal form of
the typeface is good for
giving information."*

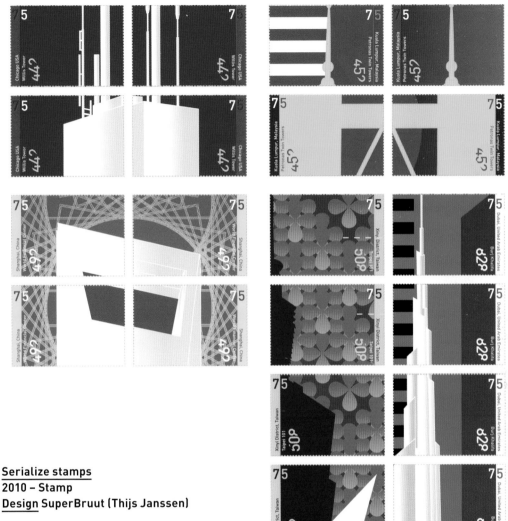

Serialize stamps
2010 – Stamp
Design SuperBruut (Thijs Janssen)

A series of stamps with the theme: the (five)
tallest buildings of the world in 2010. The
stamp sheet consists of several components of
the national flags, the illustrated buildings and
little information about the buildings. Together
they make a visual color explosion.

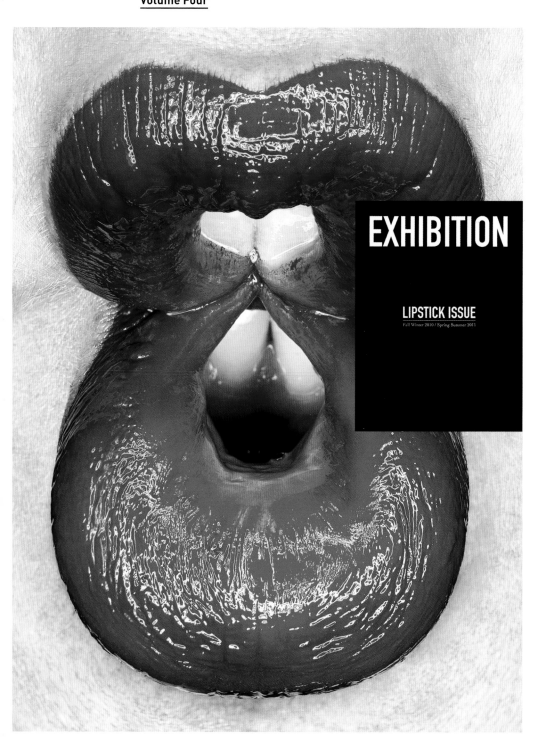

EXHIBITION

LIPSTICK ISSUE
Fall Winter 2010 / Spring Summer 2011

This is the first issue of a photography magazine focused on a unique theme: this one lipstick. Every photographer,

writer or fashion artist has the opportunity to bring his own interpretation about the topic. The layout is sober, with emphases on the powerful pictures. Each artist is introduced with a typographic composition, based on his own name letters and a particular structure that prefigure the photographic work.

Gaël Hugo & Edwin Sberro's Favorite DIN Letter is "C".

Typeface in Use
DIN 1451 Engschrift

SØLVE
SUND
SBØ

Make-up Artist VAL GARLAND

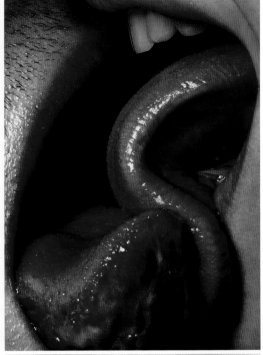

RI
CH
AR
DB
UR
BR
ID
GE

Make-up Artist PETER PHILIPS

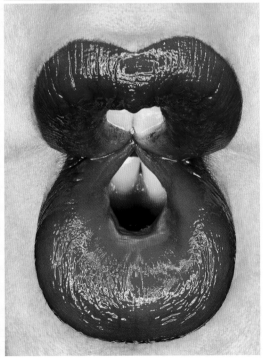

"We were looking for a condensed font, with a phallic aspect, to match the theme of this first issue of the magazine: lipstick. It will then become the global identity typeface."

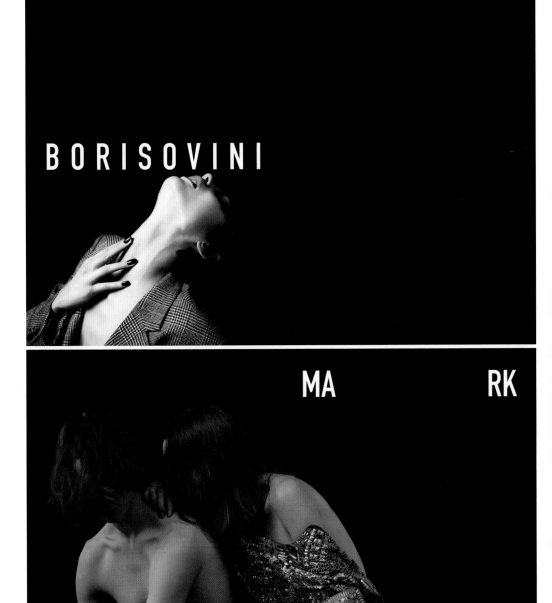

BORISOVINI

MA

RK

SEG

AL

O

Designliga's Favorite
DIN Letter is "O".

on3
2008 – Corporate Design, Poster,
Advertising Material
Client on3
Design Designliga (Andreas
Döhring)

on3 is the youth platform of the
Bavarian Broadcasting Associa-
tion. Positioned as "on3 activates
young people in Bavaria", it inte-
grates content from the fields of
media, music, culture and politics
into a single network for a target
group of young people aged from
15 to 25. Independent youth events,
TV and radio programming are
brought together under the head-
ing of on3. The element "on" is a
colloquial way of indicating the
state of being online, while "3"
stands for the three planned sec-
tors of activity of the broadcasting
company – radio, TV and Internet.
In addition, in leetspeak the figure
"3" stands for the letter "E", so
that on3 could be read as "one".
The logo accompanying the brand
was also deliberately designed to
permit multiple interpretations. For example, at second
glance it can be seen to include a USB connector, a sym-
bolic reference to the multimedia and interactive features
of on3 as a youth platform. The look and feel of the brand
communicated the brand's core idea of "activation". The
unconventional, powerful and memorable visual language
appeals to a young, self-assured target group. A compre-
hensive design manual ensures continuity in the day-to-
day use of the corporate design elements.

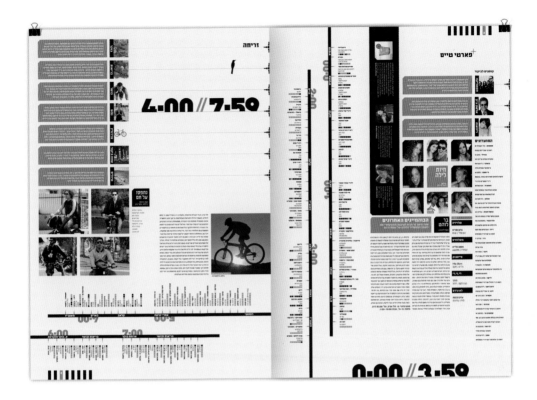

24//7
2010 – Typography, Magazine Design
Client Bezalel
Design Moshik Nadav

24//7 is a weekly magazine based in Tel Aviv (City in Israel). Tel Aviv is a city that has attractions around the clock. I used that fact and created a magazine that informs the reader about the best attractions of the city.

The reader can find his attraction by the hour of the day and by that, he can see what day the attractions occur. I used the Hebrew typeface "The Next Exit" that was inspired by the DIN Typeface.

The Magazine was printed on a News Paper in broadsheet size (spreads: 81x57 cm).

"24//7 Tel Aviv Magazine included a lot of details.
I tried to design the magazine with a fresh and
clean look that will highlight the grid and the
timeline of the magazine. This typeface is working well with my concept."

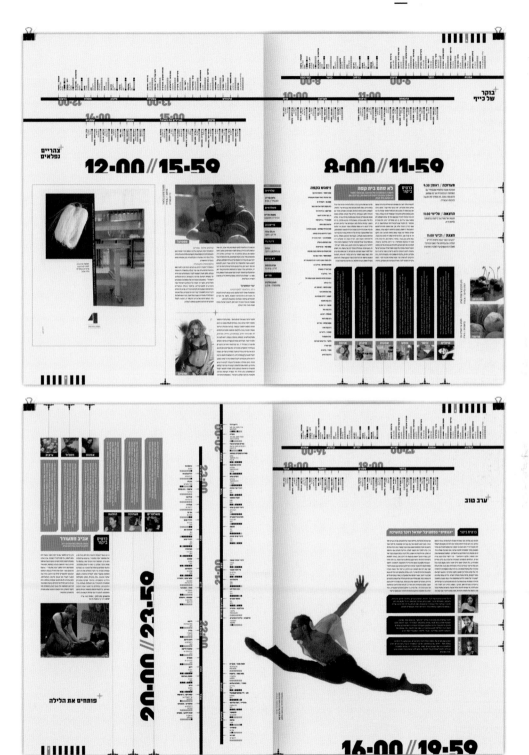

Grec 08
2008 – Event Design
Client Ajuntament de Barcelona
Design TwoPoints.Net

Grec is one of the most successful festivals in
Barcelona. Its programming is as broad as its
audience. From pop concerts to opera, theatre
and ballet, to the circus and puppet theatre,
the very diverse groups attend the Grec.

Typeface in Use
FF DIN Bold, FF DIN Light

TwoPoints.Net's
Favorite DIN Character
is "ⓐ".

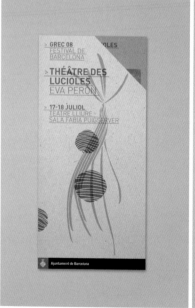

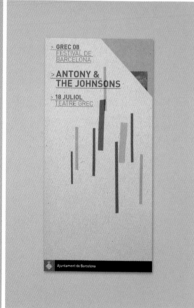

TwoPoints.Net developed a flexible, but very operative visual system which is based upon human and artistic expression as a metaphor. The visibility of the working material as paper, paint, scissors and markers creates a proximity that can be experienced in events as well as in examples of theatre or dance acts that are part of the Grec festival.

Each of the five genres became its own visual language and color code. The flexible system adapts itself quickly to each format and media, that was later used by festival organizers. It can guide or surprise the reader. It helps to distinguish between different genres and applications. It reacts to different audiences and is able to communicate with all of them.

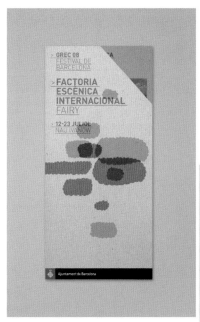

*"The FF DIN was the perfect typeface
to use in combination with the illustrations. It gave the composition
steadiness and helped to develop
a very legible structure."*

**Museu Ciències
Naturals Barcelona**
2010 – Visual Idenity
<u>Client</u> Ajuntament de Barcelona
<u>Design</u> TwoPoints.Net

The Museu de Ciències Naturals de Barcelona (Natural Science Museum of Barcelona) is changing... On one hand, most of its content dedicated to a larger audience will be moved to a new building, the Espai Blau Forum, which offers more space and possibilities (permanent exhibition space, classrooms, media-library, etc.).

On the other hand the old building of the Museum of Zoology, Castell dels Dragons will be used primarily as a documentation and research centre – with only a small part of it is going to be accessible to the public. The old Museu Martorell (Museum of Geology), will also change and mainly document the evolution of the Museu de Ciències Naturals de Barcelona (museum inside the museum) and function as a centre for the Parc de la Ciutadella (Barcelona Bioparc).

These changes will help the Museu de Ciències Naturals de Barcelona to communicate its activities more efficiently and establish its own identity, which until now has been associated with the former museums of Zoology, Geology, and the Ciutadella.

Typeface in Use
FF DIN Bold, Minion

TwoPoints.Net was invited, along with two other design firms from Barcelona, to develop a proposal for a new visual identity that would establish the brand of the Museu de Ciències Naturals de Barcelona on the four different exhibition sites.

The challenge was to create an umbrella identity for a museum with four different spaces which aren't divided by sciences, but by functions and target groups.

The 130-year history of the museum plays an important role in natural science in Catalonia. With the expansion of the exhibition venues and exhibition content, important new elements will be added to the tradition of the brand, and combine them with the vision of the future. Tradition (documentation and conservation) and innovation (research) became the key words when developing the concept for the visual identity.

"For a Graduate show that was showcasing the best new talent it felt best to represent them with a modern clean typeface and DIN was a popular choice at the time. After deliberating other typefaces to use and not wanting to go with Helvetica we settled on DIN as it had the right look for the promotion of the Graduate show."

A

Adrian Newell's Favorite DIN Letter is "A".

Graduate Showcase
2007 – Poster
Client University of Salford
Design Adrian Newell, Graeme Hale

Whilst still studying at the University of Salford myself and Graeme Hale were asked to design all the promotional material for the Graduate exhibition in 2007. As the exhibition was to take place in the Cube Gallery we decided to create various "sculptures" out of children's play cubes which were then used as a background image. Strong bold typography then complemented the images to create a strong collateral of promotional materials for the show.

University of Salford
A Greater Manchester University

Graduate
Showcase
06.06–
09.06.07

Featuring Work by

Computer & Video Games - BSc (Hons)
Design Management - BA (Hons)
Design Futures - BA (Hons)
Digital 3D Design - BA (Hons)
Fashion - BA (Hons)
Graphic Design - BA (Hons)
Graphic Design - HND
Interior Design - BA (Hons)
Product Design - BA (Hons)
Sports Equipment Design - BSc (Hons)

Private View

Thursday 7th June   5.30pm – 8.00pm

Opening Times

Wednesday 6th June 12am – 5.30pm
Thursday 7th June   12am – 5.00pm
Friday 8th June   12am – 5.30pm
Saturday 9th June   12am – 5.30pm

Venue

Cube Gallery
113 - 115 Portland Street
Manchester
M1 6FB

For more information contact:
Elesh Makwana
0161 295 6140
e.makwana@salford.ac.uk
www.artdes.salford.ac.uk

Visual Arts Degree Show

8th – 12th June   10.00am – 4.00pm

Private view

Thursday 7th June   6.00pm – 9.00pm

PLUS Exhibition: BA (Hons) Art & Design
with Foundation Year
Open Studios: MA Contemporary Fine Art.

Venue

Irwell Valley Campus
School of Art & Design
Blandford Road
Salford
M3 6BD

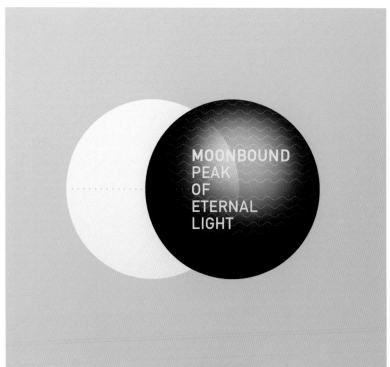

MOONBOUND
PEAK
OF
ETERNAL
LIGHT

Ritxi Ostáriz's Favorite
DIN Letter is "A".

OUR DAY WILL COME   .01
FLASH THROUGH YOUR BRAIN   .02
HEATWAVE   .03
HERE IN WONDERLAND   .04
A REASON TO HOPE   .05
PEAK OF ETERNAL LIGHT   .06
DREAMS ARE FUNNY SOMETIMES   .07
HOLD ME   .08
THE RIGHT DAY FOR GOODBYES   .09
IN THE COUNTRY OF THE BLIND   .10
HE SAYS, SHE SAYS   .11
WHILE WE SLEEP   .12

PEAK OF ETERNAL LIGHT DESCRIBES A POINT ON A BODY WITHIN THE SOLAR SYSTEM WHICH IS ETERNALLY BATHED IN
SUNLIGHT. THE MOON'S NORTH POLE MAY HAVE PERMANENTLY SUNLIT LOCATIONS, KNOWN ROMANTICALLY AS PEAKS
OF ETERNAL LIGHT.

· ·

PRODUCED BY FABIO TRENTINI, MARKUS REUTER AND PAT MASTELOTTO

MIXED BY FABIO TRENTINI AND MARKUS REUTER @ FAB LABS, BELLUNO, ITALY, AUGUST 2009

MASTERED BY LEE FLETCHER @ FLETCHERTRONICS, UK, NOVEMBER 2009

RECORDED AND ENGINEERED BY FABIO TRENTINI @ FAB LABS BETWEEN JANUARY 2008 AND JULY 2009, EXCEPT FOR
PAT MASTELOTTO'S DRUMS AND PERCUSSION RECORDED BY PAT, ASSISTED BY KENDALL ROSS CLARK @ PAT'S LOFT
IN AUSTIN, TEXAS, USA, DAVE GREGORY'S GUITARS RECORDED BY DAVE @ HIS HOME STUDIO IN SWINDON, UK, PETE
VUCKOVIC'S VOCALS RECORDED BY PETE @ HIS HOME STUDIO IN LONDON, UK, MARKUS REUTER'S TOUCH GUITARS U8
RECORDED BY MARKUS @ THE ATELIER IN INNSBRUCK, AUSTRIA, MARIO DRINKMANN'S KEYS RECORDED BY MARIO @
IM=PULS STUDIO IN MÜNSTER, GERMANY, AND JEFF COLLIER'S BACKING VOCALS RECORDED BY JEFF @ HIS HOME
STUDIO IN BERLIN, GERMANY

ARTWORK BY RITXI OSTÁRIZ, WWW.RITXIOSTARIZ.COM

FABIO USES: 56L BASSES, EPIFANI BASS AMPS, ANDREA AGNOLETTO @ HAMICHORD/CRUMAR (CRUMER/MFB
CUSTOM BASS PEDALS) ARNE VON BRILL @ TARANAKI GUITARS, GERMANY (EASTWOOD BASSES, PIOTRONIX AND
DIAMOND STOMP-BOXES), ROMAN MAGIS @ MAGIS AUDIOBAU, GERMANY (VINTAGEDESIGN OUTBOARD GEAR, PELUSO
MICROPHONES), PETER LAGEMANN @ S.E.A. VERTRIEB & CONSULTING, GERMANY (UNIVERSAL AUDIO UAD-2) AND
GIANNI ROCCI @ ROD'S GARAGE, ITALY (DRUMADOG) FOR THEIR SUPPORT.

FABIO WOULD LIKE TO EXPRESS HIS GRATITUDE TO:
HIS WIFE FOR HER ENDLESS LOVE AND PATIENCE - MARKUS AND PAT FOR TOO MANY THINGS TO MENTION - HIS
BUDDY MODO BIERKAMP FOR BEING THERE ANYTIME, HELPING HIM IN MANY WAYS - DAVE GREGORY FOR HIS BRILLI-
ANT CONTRIBUTION AND HIS KINDNESS - MICHI DEI ROSSI AND LE ORME - HIS FAVOURITE PUNK ROCK VOCALIST/BASS
PLAYER PETE VUCKOVIC - MARIO BRINKMANN AND HIS BEAUTIFUL, ANALOG WORLD - HIS GOOD FRIEND JEFF 'THE
GARBAGE MAN' COLLIER FOR HIS AWESOME LYRICS AND THE IDEA OF COVERING THE BLUE NILE SONG 'HEATWAVE' -
NICK SIMCOCK FOR ENGLISH COACHING, FOR HIS COOL RADIO INTERVIEWS AND FOR BEING 'THE MAN ON THE PHONE'
- BERNHARD WÖSTHEINRICH & YOSHI HAMPL @ UNSUNG RECORDS - THE MULTITALENTED LEE FLETCHER - PAOLO
AND FRANCESCO VETTORELLO FOR MAKING THEIR HOUSE AVAILABLE FOR SOME RECORDINGS - PAOLO FILIPPI @ CAVO
STUDIO, BERGAMO, ITALY FOR SUPPORT AND FRIENDSHIP - HIS SLOVENIAN FRIENDS ZARE PAK, NIKOLA SEKULOVIC
AND DAN-D - HIS PUBLISHER TOM NEVERMANN @ AMV-TALPA... AND ANYONE HE MIGHT HAVE FORGOTTEN.

WWW.MYSPACE.COM/MOONBOUNDMUSIC - WWW.UNSUNG-RECORDS.COM

*"We wanted a typography that worked perfectly on capital
letters, and gave a touch of modernity but also elegance
to the design."*

Moonbound. Peak of Eternal Light
2010 – Music Packaging
Client Fabio Trentini and
Markus Reuter
Design Estudio Ritxi Ostáriz

Art direction and design of the
second album by the Italian artist
Fabio Trentini (Moonbound), produced by Markus Reuter. The title
of the album, a "Peak of Eternal
Light", is a point on a body within
the Solar System which is eternally
bathed in sunlight. We tried to represent this concept on the design
by using black, white and yellow,
and the mixing of different graphic
symbols as points and waves (wave
+ particle = light), and the symbol
of infinite (eternity).

*"DIN's highly geo-
metric design with
no contrast between
the stems, and its
90° angles, is a
perfect match for
Elma's angular and
hard-edged sound."*

Elma no MIS
2010 – Poster
Client Elma / MIS - Museu da Imagem e do Som
Design Guilherme Falcão

Elma is a Brazilian experimental metal band.
Their music is influenced by other experimental acts, such as Sonic Youth, Sunnn O))), and
Melvins. Their emphasis on repetitive struc-
tures and a tight rhythm section is echoed in
the posters repetition of the band's name,
coupled with other geometric shapes such
as a triangle and a bar. Although it is never
spelled completely, its is readable somehow.
The poster was screen-printed in black on
black paper, achieving a very glossy and
thick texture.

Guilherme Falcão's
Favorite DIN Letter
is "M".

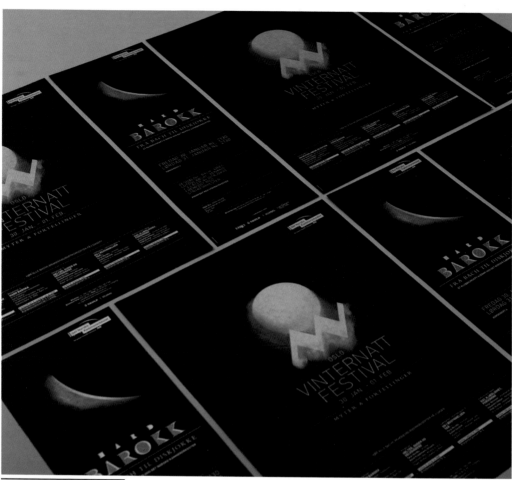

Neue Design's Favorite
DIN Letter is "Ø".

Oslo Winter Night Festival / Oslo Vinternatt Festival
2009 – Event Identity
Client Norwegian Chamber Orchestra
Design Neue Design Studio

Oslo Winter Night Festival is a classical music festival, and
the concept for 2009 was "myths and stories". The illustrations with their eerie glow are elements found in the logo,
and resemble shapes which can be seen during northern
winter nights. The illustrations were painted with water-
color, and then scanned and adjusted. All elements where
silkscreen-printed in silver on black cardboard.

*"DIN is the corporate font for the Norwegian
Chamber Orchestra. Its geometric structure
and many weights used in combination with
Bembo let us achieve both harmony and contrast; equally important in the classical music
the orchestra perform."*

Typeface in Use
DIN Light, DIN Regular, DIN
Medium, DIN Bold, DIN Black
PF DIN Display Extra Thin
Bembo Std Regular

'0'
2008 – Typographic Treatment, Poster
Design Graphics Designed (Jack Crossing)

Typeface in Use
DIN

A typographic exploration into legibility, using
type and image.

99 100
2007 – Book
Client Krabbesholm
Højskole, Denmark
Design Gunmad

Celebrating the hundred years of the Danish "Folke-højskole" Krabbesholm. The school started as a traditional Danish folk high school, but is now a well known art school with preparatory classes in art, architecture and design. Even though Krabbesholm is located on the Danish countryside, the school has a dynamic contemporary environment with guest teachers from home and abroad. The book features historical text as well as contributions in form of essays, poems and artwork. Conceptually the book focuses on the school's shift from 99 to 100 years of age and visualizes the change the school has gone through.

Typeface in Use
DIN

Medens skolen i Jebjerg havde været en helt traditionel skole for landboungdommen, skulle Krabbesholm nu være en skole for hele folket, og alligevel var det umgdommen i Dorfs indvielsestale, der skulle føres ud »... ikke i kritikkens hængedynd, men på det positives klippegrund.« Dorf lagde vægt på, at skolen skulle imødekomme »... den trang, der er for hånden, men den skal ikke nedlægge de våben, hvormed den har kæmpet og sejret.« De våben var først og fremmest det levende ord, der »... kan vække samtidig med, at det kan oplive.« Axelsen talte naturligvis også og kom med følgende markante ord: »Højskolen skal vise vejen opad, stille de store krav frem, bringe lys, give kundskab ved siden af og vise, hvorledes det skal leves og ægte menneskeliv i pagt med ånd – af Guds nåde til Guds ære ...« og dermed »... få et velsignet arbejde gjort for dansk åndsliv.« Intet mindre. Kristian Schultz-Petersen betegner Axelsen som »... en from mand med fuld tillid til instamen over sig, sådan som en forstander skal være.«[2]

Man mere end ærer en uvilje mod det moderne gennembrud (»kritikkens hængedynd«) og den sækularisering, som Brandes havde introduceret i 1870erne. Ja, Axelsen gik så vidt som at sige, at om man gav afkald på det grundtvigske livs- og kristensyn, han op havde berettet om, så var højskolens tid omme.

Højskolens budskab og situation var vanskelig. På næsten alle sider var den ongardet af folk, der tænkte anderledes. Socialismen og arbejderbevægelsen, det nævnte moderne gennembrud og Højre, der endnu ikke havde antaget navnet konservativt folkeparti. Bondekulturen, der

igennem 1870erne og 1880erne havde skabt meget nyt og først og fremmest bidraget til såvel åndeligt som økonomisk og organisatorisk at løfte dansk landbrug, var puffet noget i baggrunden af industriens og dermed byernes eksplosive vækst. Derved kom højskolen, nok mere end den selv mente, til at fremstå som noget indadvendt, tilbageskuende og traditionsbundet. På den baggrund kunne Axelsen næppe annoncere andet, end han gjorde. Ikke mindst i betragtning af, at han næppe længere besad den pionerånd, der i samarbejde med pastor Kr. Glad i 1884 havde skabt højskolen i Jebjerg.

I 1910 stiftedes højskoleforeningen, der overtog skolens ejendom. Økonomien holdt ikke til de store mål og de fejende økonomiske håndbevægelser. Axelsen forsvandt til Sjælland og Dorf'erne tog til bage til USA. Skolen fortsatte i Skive. Og med den i 1907 oprettede håndværkerskole, der lidt på samme familievis blev ledet af Johanne og Jens Bundgaard i nært samarbejde med højskolen. I en kort periode var Krabbesholm endda ledet herfra, da det var ved at gå helt galt med økonomien og de hastigt skiftende forstandere.

Efter adskillige forstanderskifter kommer Krabbesholm i 1925 endelig ind i en mere rolig periode. Anders Vedel som allerede var et kendt navn i højskolekredse, blev forstander. Med Vedel sker der en afgørende vending i skolens orientering. Hidtil var Krabbesholm udpræget en egnshøjskole, hvis grundsubstans var egnen og dens folkelige og kirkelige liv. Elevgrundlaget var som altid landbrugets karle og piger. Vedel ændrer ikke på det, men åbner for en ny dimension: Den mellemfolkelige. Og Ikke alene det. Han deltager i tidens pædagogiske debat

om folkeskolen, hvor folkeskoleloven af 1937 diskuteres i forhold til det landsbyordnede skolevæsen, der i sit tankesæt og sine undervisningsidealer kom tættere på det grundtvigske i modsætning til det købstadsordnede skolevæsen. Vedel er ikke så bekymret for, at faglighed skal fortrænge opdragelsesopgaven, og peger på, at det kan folk selv få indflydelse på og tage stilling til. Selvom han ikke er tilhænger af de nye centralskoler (skoleforbundene), så udelukker han ikke, at de også kan anvendes, hvis man ikke glemmer den rette sammenhæng mellem lærerens rolle som kulturformidler og forældrenes tillid til, at skolen også formidler den kultur.[3]

Han rejser efter den tids forhold ganske meget. Norge, England, Australien, hvor han endda bliver æresdoktor. Han har senere hen i Japan, kontakter i Tyskland og optræder ved alle mulige indenlandske lejligheder. Markant siger han fra på et højskolemøde i 1934, hvor usikre højskolefolk skulle forholde sig til Hitlers magtovertagelse i Tyskland og følger op hjemme i Skive og i Højskolebladet. Politik bliver med Vedel en del af det nødvendige folkelige engagement.

Han overtager efter en forstanderstilling ved Roskilde Højskole en skole, der var i knæ rent økonomisk. Ukendt med egnen var han ikke. Hans første arbejde som højskolelærer var hos Axelsen i Jebjerg – i øvrigt kort før flytningen til Skive. Hertil kom, at Vedel som højskolemand repræsenterede en analytisk tankegang af sjældent format. Han formåede på én gang at samle det lokalt forankrede folkelige oplysningsarbejde med det internationalt kristiske udsyn og dets folkelige gennembrud. Det skete gennem en Grundtvig-forståelse af et næsten moderne tilsnit.

I essayet Det Folkelige' fra 1928 sammensætter han begrebet af forskellige elementer. Dels optagetheden af, hvad der hænder folket, som noget, der angår hver enkelt, dels Jakob Knudsens opdeling af begrebet i det populære og det nationale, som Vedel forkaster med den bemærkning, at Knudsen mangler »...et udtryk for fællesskabet, det vi som folk, som danske er fælles om, har eller kan have med hinanden.« Herfra går den lige linje til Grundtvigs digt: Folkeligt skal alt nu være. Og dermed får han slået fast, at bestemmelsen af det folkelige ikke er nogen enkel sag. Grundtvig havde jo unægtelig sine problemer med begrebet. Han har siger, at »Til et folk de alle høre, som sig regner selv dertil, har for modersmålet øre, har for fædrelandet ild.« Grundtvig sender så sige forståelsen af udtrykket tilbage

---

RID= DER= SALEN

ARKI- TEK- TU- REN PÅ KRAB- BES- HOLM

Af højskolelærer Helene Stigel

Tiden går sin gang og afsætter sine arkitektoniske spor. Krabbesholm Højskole har mærker efter disse aftryk – og dagligt bevæger vi os rundt i fortidens bygninger samtidig med, at vi er fremadrettede og sorger mye av på nutidens arkitekturens vasen. Vi trives godt i dette miskmask af huse og bygninger, som har en særlig sjæl og atmosfære.

Når man som elev første gang mødes med dette sted, er det selvfølgelig arkitekturen og omgivelserne, som sætter sig på nethinden. Derefter er det selve livet og dagligdagen på stedet, der bliver erindringen om stedet og dets udvikling.

Hvad er så det særlige ved Krabbesholm Højskoles bygninger? Det er den med særlige atmosfæren og stemning med sit nyt og gammelt lever side om side og ikke skubber til hinanden, men derimod understøtter og holder sammen på hinanden.

Det er den svær og besværlig balance, husene skal have til hinanden. Hovedbygningen og længerne danner gårdspladsen, som er stedets centrum. Derudfra spredes bygningerne sådan lidt kaotisk og tilfældigt. Men der er en overordnet plan. Den kan være svær at finde i stålhøjde, men ser man på området fra 500 meters højde, ligner stedet en lille landsby; med det centrale torv, beboelse, gader og flankeret af skov, marker og vand.

Alt det er netop, hvad vi oplever. En lille landsby. Et sted, hvor man vandrer fra rum til rum – udendørs såvel som indendørs – og opsnapper samtaler om livet om kunsten. En lille landsby befolket af hovedsagelig unge, energiske og tolerante personer, der har det tilfælles, at de har en

hverdag, der skal leves sammen.

At stedet Krabbesholm har en lang og en lille smule blodig historie – med spøgelse og grumme fruentimmer – bør også give et historisk vingesus hos os alle, der bor og lever her. Vi befinder os godt i hovedbygningen, der er 500 år gammel. Riddersalen danner ramme om mangt og meget. Vi kan godt fornemme tiden her; arbødigheden for rummets kraft og dominans. Her har været elever i 100 år. Der er blevet lyttet og hørt lidt af hvert.

Vi spiser og fester i spisesalen – en stadsbygning fra 1760erne. Ombygget naturligvis, men der ånes går i lavt lange, lavloftede rum. Og så er der elevværelserne, spredt her og der.

Alle har de deres historie. Nogle er tidligere pigekamre, udbygget og moderniseret af kunstnere, arkitekter og designere, der har skabt en historie om det at bo sammen to og to. Andre huses i sortmalede, barakfligende huse, hvor man enkeltvis lever side om side med hinanden, og hvor man deler en kande kaffe i et lille fælterum med ildelugtende secondhand-sofaer.

Så er der undervisningslokalerne. Dem er der mange af, og de er lige så forskellige som alt det andet.

Der er højloftede lokaler til kunstundervisningen – det var jo højskolens gymnasiikstal engang. En bygning fra 1960erne. Der er scenen, der i dag bruges til grafisk design, med det store vindue ud til vandet og alt det nye.

I håndværkerskolen fra århundredeskiftet huses i stueplan faget design, og arkitekturholdet er placeret i husets tagetage. Der er blevet renoveret og flyttet rundt på fagskaberne, og nye er kommet til.

For nogle år siden besluttede vi at tilp

**Gunmad's Favorite DIN
Number is "0".**

*"The DIN typeface is the typeface
always used by the client for
identity means. It's often seen in
small caps, for this publication we
decided to use it in large-caps."*

The sun here reminds me of California. Berlin was really amazing, but I'm glad to be back. One of the students told me that Krabbesholm can start to feel like the only place in the entire universe. And it sort of does at times like this. I like losing track of days here. So far, I'm only responsible for showing up to breakfast and the morning meeting, lunch and dinner. I come back here to Pauls house at the end of the day to have a whisky and watch the clouds turn pink, and listen to the ravens. If I was able to live my entire life this way, I imagine I would produce a lot of work. Eventually. Or maybe not. It's so amazing to have all this time, to feel like I've disappeared for a bit. It's a light, cozy feeling that I haven't experienced for a while. I'm not sure what kind of work will come out of so much comfort. Everyone here is really great. I am looking forward to working with the students. The ones I've talked with seem really smart and interesting. I better get something together to teach. Maybe that will give me some ideas of my own ... or maybe not, I'm lazy. I'm going to enjoy the luxury of this laziness while I'm here.

Maybe I'll make some monument to laziness, or paranoia. I love this house, but when I stand up in the tub in the cold morning to shower, I feel a bit exposed with all the windows. It's so quiet here too. It's nice, but I'm not used to it. It's like if I talk in my sleep, I'll wake everyone up in the dorm next door. They'll all laugh at me at breakfast. Everyone will know I don't have any ideas. One of the students asked me in Berlin if I felt any pressure to produce something while I was here and I smiled and said wise, of course not. Although I really feel like I should do something. I'm being treated so well. It will be good to work with the students. Something will come of that, I guess. Something always comes, eventually. Usually.

I think I'll have just one more whiskey before it gets dark. To toast the doves and ravens, to the frogs in my bathtub, and a big toast to these lazy days that go by softly and blend into each other like a warm, slow blue.

Invitation Diplôme
2007 – Invitation
Client EPSAA
Design Superatelier (Mathieu Mandin)

It was in Mathieu Mandin's last academic year
in EPSAA where his design proposal was
chosen as the final invitation solution for the
school's degree show. The invites were silk-
screened on thick tracing paper by Atelier
Patatnik.

*"I chose DIN here for its thinness
and elegance which matched the
thread-like links between graphic
shapes and names and contrasted
with the massive black Helvetica
used in the background."*

Superatelier's Favorite
DIN Letter is "a".

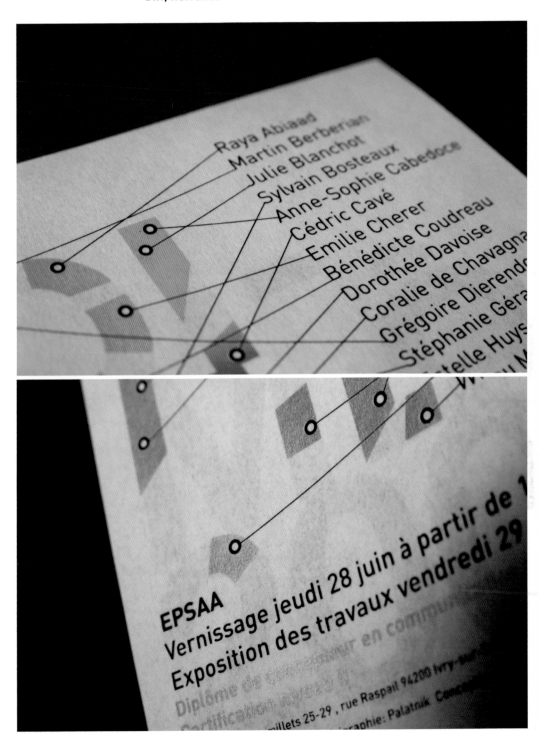

Raya Abiaad
Martin Berberian
Julie Blanchot
Sylvain Bosteaux
Anne-Sophie Cabedoce
Cédric Cavé
Emilie Cherer
Bénédicte Coudreau
Dorothée Davoise
Coralie de Chavagna
Grégoire Dierend
Stéphanie Géra
stelle Huys

EPSAA
Vernissage jeudi 28 juin à partir de 1
Exposition des travaux vendredi 29
Diplôme de concepteur en commun
Certification niveau II
illets 25-29 , rue Raspail 94200 Ivry-su
raphie: Palatnik Cons

Sternstunden eines Mäzens
2008 – Exhibition Graphics
Client Staatsbibliothek zu Berlin
Design L2M3 (Sascha Lobe, Oliver Wörle)
Collaborator buerozentral.architekten,
Berlin, Germany (architects)
Photography L2M3 (Udo Meinel)

The exhibition "Sternstunden eines Mäzens – Briefe von Galilei bis Einstein" is devoted to the collector and patron of the arts Ludwig Darmstaedter. It showcases a selection of sixty autographs by famous figures from the world of science, art, literature and history.

Collecting, ordering, archiving are the keywords of the exhibition. The 60 selected autographs are accompanied by 1250 mounted sheets: The exhibition logo symbolizes the Darmstaedter Archive, at the same time creating a paper surface that provides a haptic experience. Printed on two sides, this information source also offers an economical, modest lesson of sophisticated and yet pragmatic elegance.

The catalogue is also a compilation: Consisting of individual sheets, it allows the incorporation of further transcription and commentary sheets that may be added to the book.

"The no-frills, impersonal DIN font stands for structure and order and constitutes a maximum contrast to handwriting. "

<u>How To Build a Time Capsule</u>
<u>2007 – Book Design</u>
<u>Design</u> Guilherme Falcão

Approximately one year after finishing my
graduation project, I collected all the leftover
materials and ephemera produced and collected during its development and organized
them in this volume. Divided into 5 chapters,
the book presents all those materials organized chronologically, a reproduction of the
research journal, and an index. The dust-jacket
doubles as a poster, displaying all materials
in scale and organized chronologically as they
were produced.

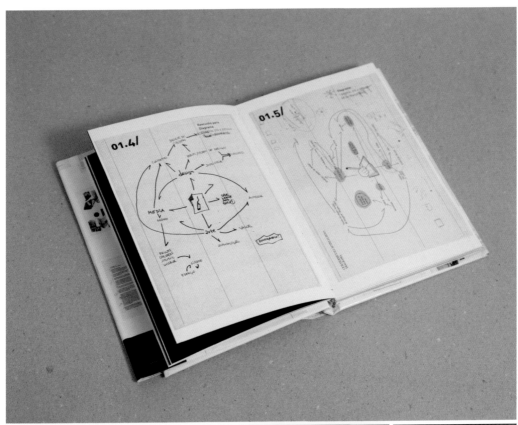

Guilherme Falcão's
Favorite DIN Letter
is "M".

Typeface in Use
DIN

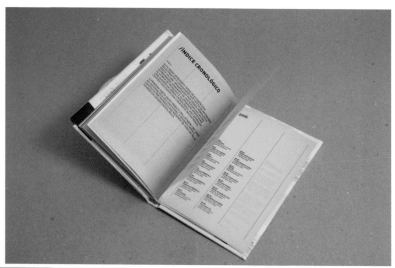

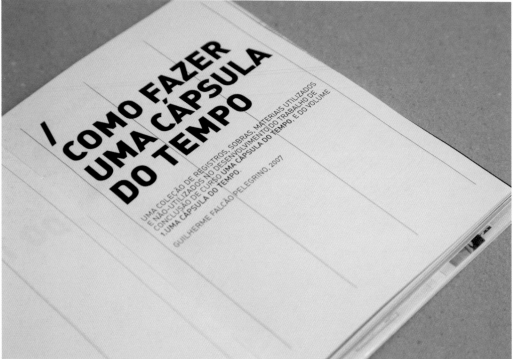

"This book is in fact a very rational and organized catalog system for several ephemera, where all the text and information is designed as an extra layer of information. Even thought it was originally drawn in the 1930s, DIN's geometric design still looks very contemporary today, and is easily recognizable in the middle of all the different content presented in the book."

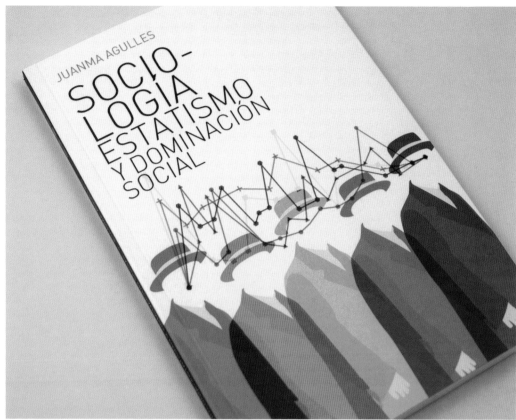

Sociología, estatismo y dominación social
2010 – Book Cover
Client Publisher Brulot
Design Nano Torres

The book writer assures in his essay that sociology is a science used as a social control tool. Starting from that concept, the designer designed the cover with color codes and graphic elements commonly used in sociology. The use of the DIN typeface for the title of the book and the writer's name, results in a balanced composition between both, the graphical and typographical parts of the cover.

Typeface in Use
FF DIN Regular

Nano Torres's Favorite
DIN Letter is "G".

Livret de l'étudiant 2008/2009
2008 – Editorial Project
Client École des beaux-arts de
Rennes
Design Caroline Fabès

The brochure for the Rennes
School of Art contains a huge
quantity of text information without any images. The most difficult
part was to "make it simple and
easy to access". I used colored
paper to make it easier for the
reader to know where the four
big parts (first year, art option,
communication option and design
option) were in the brochure.

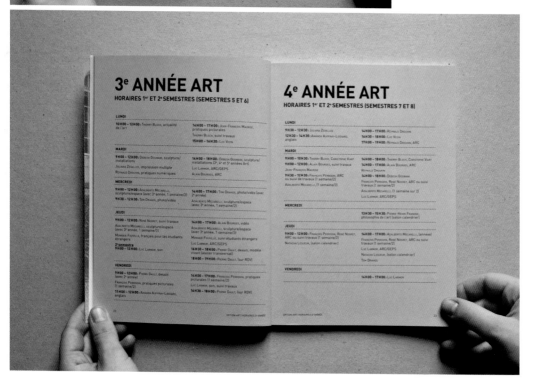

O

Caroline Fabès's Favorite DIN Letter is "O".

*"I wanted to have
a strong contrast
between titles and text.
So I used a fat black
typeface (DIN) and a
classic serif typeface
(Plantin)."*

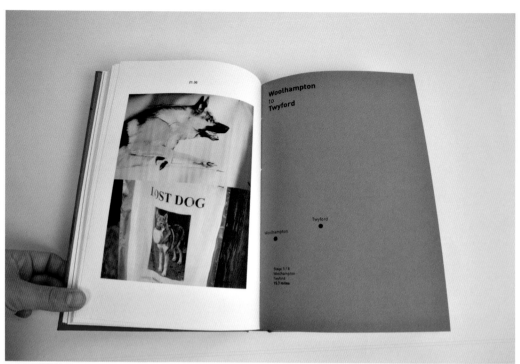

Typeface in Use   *"A favorite of mine for a personal*
DIN Pro Medium, DIN Pro Light   *project. "*

m

Joe Hinder's Favorite
DIN Letter is "m".

Bath to London Walking
2009 – Book
Design Joe Hinder
Illustration Patch Keyes

A book documenting my walk from Bath to London,
England. Each page represents 15 minutes of the 39
hour journey.

Typeface in Use
DIN Pro Medium,
DIN Pro Light

"Needed a simple font that didn't over power the illustrations."

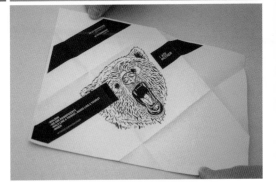

I Ate Mother EP
2009 – CD packaging
Client I Ate Mother (Band)
Design Joe Hinder
Illustration Patch Keyes

Demo EP artwork for Oxford band I Ate
Mother. Each cover is made from a folded
A4 sheet which is fastened by a sticker
that wraps around to the front cover.

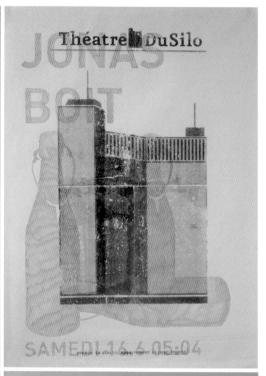

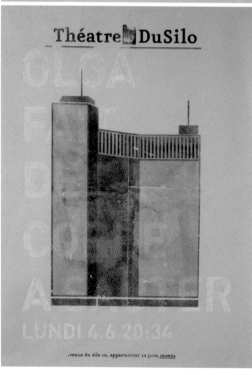

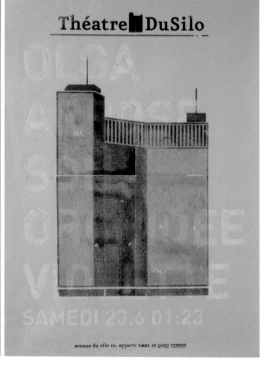

Theatre Du Silo
2008 – Poster, Visual Identity
Design Didier Quarroz at ECAL

I got the assignment to chose a place who's having a problem and to find a graphical solution to solve it.

The place I chose was the area where I was living in Ren-
ens, the problem was that people could look inside all the
apartments. There were no plants who were big enough
to obstruct passers-by's view into the residents' homes.
To use this curiosity of people in a good way, I created a
theatre, which should centre all the attention away from
all apartments to one – our apartment. I was living with
Jonas, Vincenz and Olga. We were the main actors, playing
our daily routine roles for the curios public. To announce
those daily activities I designed handmade posters, which
should be hung in the neighbourhood. On these posters
were the 'who', 'what', 'when' of the activities, in type or
in simple pictographs.

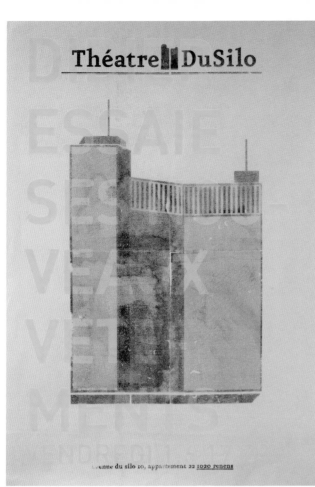

Typeface in Use
DIN Black

D

Didier Quarroz's
Favorite DIN Letter
is "D".

"I liked the constructed, geometrical and rational form of the font, which got a little bit of humanity while drawn by hand."

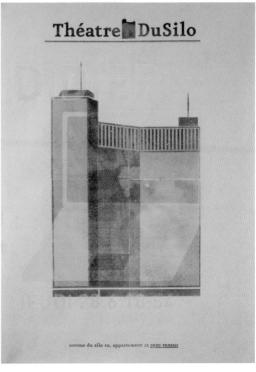

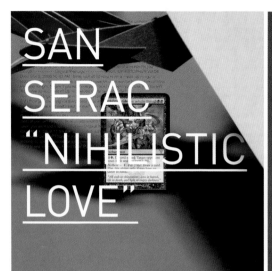

SAN
SERAC
"NIHILISTIC
LOVE"

Morning
"Dream
Palace"

KITTENZ
"M-M-M-M-
MAGIC WHI-
STLE? MA-
GIC MISSLE!

WHITE

Record Design System
2008 – Packaging
Design Chris Sherron Studio

Five record sleeves for music by my friends using systems
and chance operations, including random Google image
searches, dropping objects in front of cameras and text
from emails and Facebook conversations.

Young Male "On Automatic"

Typeface in Use
DIN Pro Regular,
DIN Pro Medium

"It is robust and distinct enough to work in a complex visual system."

Typeface in Use
DIN Condensed

Underbau's Favorite
DIN Letter is "Q".

"We needed a powerful typeface that allows us to create an image between text and picture."

De tinta y luz.
Una mirada al alma de las letras hispanoamericanas.
2010 – Book, Poster, Design Exhibition
Client Instituto Cervantes
Design underbau
Photography Daniel Mordzinski

De Tinta y Luz is still an itinerant exposition of the Argentine photographer Daniel Mordzinski, popular for his portraits of the world's most famous writers. We were interested in continuing and maintaining that text/image duality that occurs in the work of Daniel for the development of graphics. That's why we used DIN Condensed. We composed an image playing with letters, so the graphics also reflect the duality text/image.

Das neue Brandenburg
2007 – Exhibition Design, Print Design
Client Ministry for Infrastructure and Regional Planning of
the State of Brandenburg
Design Blotto Design, Michael Buhr (architect),
Kapok Architects
Photography Ingo Knies

Blotto Design's
Favorite DIN Letter
is "e".

The client needed a low-cost, modular exhibition which
could be shown in many different sites across Germany
over a period of 12 months. The challenge was to produce
a system of furniture which was light and robust, and easy
to dismantle and reassemble. The final design had to be
aesthetically and technically self-sufficient, so that it was
completely independent of the surrounding architecture.

MIT SEINEN WIDER!
LASSENSCHAFTEN
HUNDERT VERFÜGT
EINE HERAUSFORD
LANDSCHAFT. IN IH
AUS DER ZEIT DER
DIE KLASSISCHE M
DERE STELLUNG EI
BAUWERKEN, DIE S
«NEUES BRANDENE
VERDANKT DIE HEU
IHRE SPRACHE.

"In the context of post-reunification architecture in the state of Brandenburg, the use of FF DIN references the historical aspects of German engineering and technology. On a functional level, the typeface offers a broad range of weights useful for the structuring of heterogeneous information. The 'Black Alternate' cut of FF DIN is used as a weighty counterpoint to the conscious utilisation of white space. Despite its rational geometric rigor, this particular cut also has enough eccentric details to prevent it from being completely sterile."

Typeface in Use
FF DIN

This is not a touchscreen
2007 – Communication Concept for a Confer-
ence on Interaction Design
Client University of Applied Sciences, Potsdam
Design formdusche (Svenja von Döhlen, Tim
Finke, Steffen Wierer)

"This is not a touchscreen" is the leitmotif for
the conference "Innovationsforum Interaktionsdesign". The Touchscreen is an object,
which leads clearly to the point of interface
design. By matching interface design-terms
on real objects and situations, we developed
a simple "this is not-principle, which gives
you an idea of interface design an invites you
to play with it. These principle gets us over the
antagonism to explain interaction with "classic" print media. Each "This is not" - phrase
relates to interface design and at the same
time interacts with the medium, on which it
is written.

G

formdusche's Favorite
DIN Letter is "G".

Typeface in Use
DIN (headline),
Dolly (copy),
Magda (body)

INNOVATIONSFORUM
INTERAKTIONSDESIGN
⬐⬎ Potsdam, 30. + 31.03.2007
The conference on Interaction Design
Organised by the Interface Design programme
University of Applied Sciences Potsdam
Veranstaltet vom Studiengang Interface Design
der FH Potsdam | innoforum@fh-potsdam.de
http://interface.fh-potsdam.de/innoforum

This is not a touchscreen.

This is design.

This is interaction design.

Typeface in Use
DIN Black Alternate

"To communicate 'interaction' with non-inter-active media, our goal was to create a mostly 'undesigned' look in the first place. In Germany the DIN-typeface is often used in a common con-text, for example street sign. This is why it fits perfectly to our intention mentioned above."

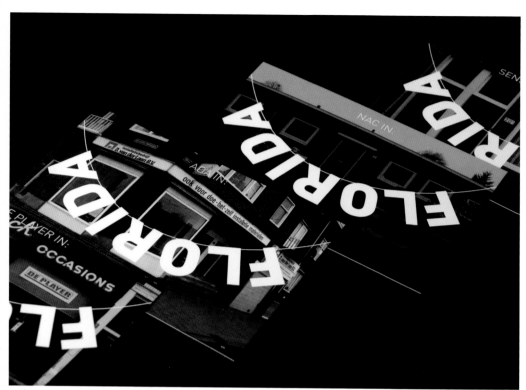

Typeface in Use
DIN

Florida
2010 – Exhibition Design, Promotional Materials
Client Tent, Rotterdam
Design StudioSpass (Jaron Korvinus & Daan Mens)

Florida is a long-term research project in which **TENT**
examines the significance of art and culture for the climate
for setting up in South Rotterdam. How is art settling into
this changing district, where is it flourishing and why?
What effect does the growing cultural infrastructure have
on South Rotterdam? Florida seeks out the physical and
digital connections and relationships; and asks how art can
contribute to the visibility of its cultural infrastructure.

*"DIN is a very clear and informative
typeface which was perfect for this
exhibition."*

Vor 100 Jahren schenkte Ludwig Darmstaedter der Königlichen Bibliothek seine Autographen- sammlung. Die Staatsbibliothek zu Berlin ehrt ihren großen Mäzen mit dieser Ausstellung.

60 Dokumente der berühmtesten Persönlichkeiten aus Wissen- schaft, Kunst, Literatur und Geschichte sind Beispiele für die Universalität der über 250.000 Dokumente umfassenden Sammlung.

3

L2M3's Favorite
DIN Number is "3".

"The DIN font fits the industrial con-
text of the Ruhr Museum in terms
of subject matter and form. It is
also the font used in the corporate
design of the Zollverein coal mine."

Ruhrmuseum Essen
2010 – Exhibition Graphics
Client Stiftung Zollverein Essen
Design L2M3 (Sascha Lobe, Frank Geiger, David Arzt)
Architecture hg merz
Photography Brigida Conzalez

One part of the Zollverein Coal Mine world cultural heritage site is the former coal wash plant converted by Rem
Kohlhaas, that has housed the Ruhr Museum since January
2010. Visitors experience a succession of very different
impressions and discover an equally chequered history.
The visual identity in the form of DNA code is constituted
by a typographical system that imprints itself in different
aggregate states into the exhibition. Based on the idea of
a mine car or container, the individual words sit more or
less exactly in a grid system of areas. This gives rise to a
rhythm that appears mechanical and which is formulated
in the form of graphics and objects.

Typeface in Use
DIN Regular, DIN Light, DIN Bold

EGO
2008 – Environmental Graphics
Client Osaka University of Arts
Design kokokumaru Inc (Yoshimaru Takahashi)

Stretching widely across the floor, ECO can be seen from anywhere in the hall, but when the observer stands on one specific point, the letters seem to stand vertically in the middle of the hall. The type indicates how closely the condition of the ecology is connected to the egoistic behaviour of humankind.

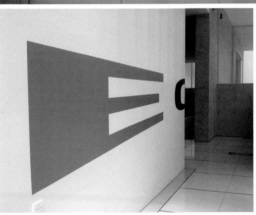

ECO^2
2007 – Environmental Graphics
Client Osaka University of Arts
Design kokokumaru Inc (Yoshimaru Takahashi)

Only from one point the word ECO2 can be seen
in its complete two-dimensional form. From
any other perspective it grows and skews
in three dimensions. By merging the words
ECO and CO2 we want to show how much one
depends on the other.

*"I chose DIN for the ECO project
because this typeface has no
organic lines and in itself trans-
ports no emotion."*

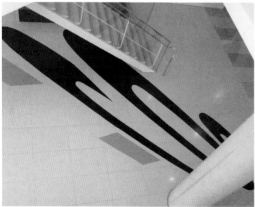

Schauraum4
2010 – Exhibition Graphics, Signage
Client University of Applied Sciences and Arts
in Dortmund, Germany
Design Marvin Boiko
Photography Philip Kirstner
Event-team Sandra Birkner, Marvin Boiko,
Jennifer Braun, Martin Demmer, Annika Feuss,
Mailin Lemke, Martin Mascheski, Sebastian
Müller, Jana Pechan, Jan Rocho, Vera Schäper,
Caroline Seidel, Anna Wunderle

"Schauraum4" is an exhibition that shows the
final projects of the Graphic Design, Photography, Object and Spatial Design and Film Camera disciplines over a period of three days at
the University of Applied Sciences and Arts in
Dortmund, Germany.

K

Marvin Boiko's
Favorite DIN Letter
is "K".

Typeface in Use
DIN 1451
Mittelschrift

"DIN Mittelschrift is used within the corporate design of the University of
Applied Sciences and Arts Dortmund. The school has a strong focus on
multidisciplinary, which was our initial point for the design system. The
students can pick different skills from the disciplines Graphic Design,
Photography, Object and Spatial Design and Film Camera to gain their
competence. Due to this aspect, the capital letter represent the different
departments of the University of Applied Sciences and Arts Dortmund.
Each letter is disassembled and newly combined which leads to the several patterns. This system symbolizes the individuality of our students."

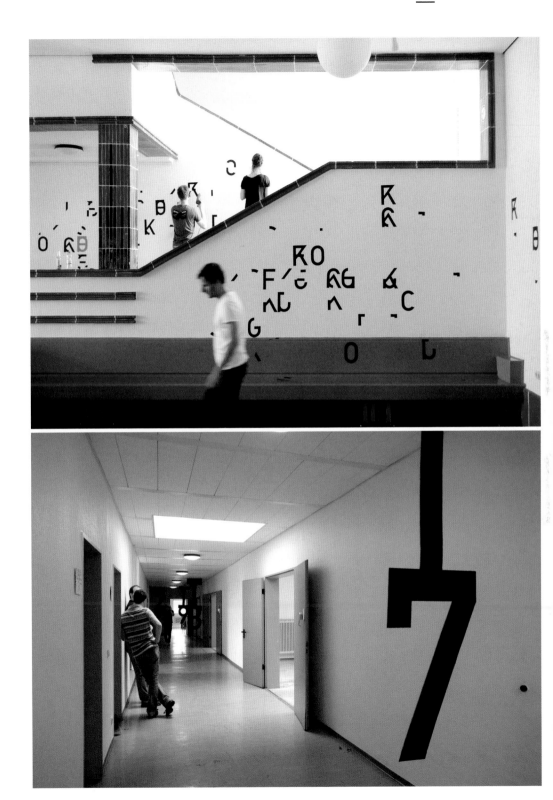

includes art direction and design for magazines and events, branding and identity, and websites.
-pp. 100-101

formdusche
www.formdusche.de

Comprised of four graphic designers, Svenja von Döhlen, Steffen Wierer, Tim Finke, and Timo Hummel, formdusche is active in the broad field of communications design. Ever since its inception in 2004 formdusche's main vision, plain and simple, has been to conceive individual answers for each client's tasks. Both, listen to the client and form follows content, rank on top of their design philosophy charts. As their work is concept-driven, they like to irritate with typographic ideas or to find simple solutions for complex processes. formdusche's focus lies on corporate design, typography, book and editorial design, illustration, and communications strategies.
-pp. 136-139

Gaël Hugo, Edwin Sberro
www.exhibition-magazine.com

Exhibition is a brand new creative platform driven by a collective of four people: Edwin Sberro, Gaël Hugo, Boris Ovini and Jean-Christophe Husson. The product of their collaboration is an annual concept magazine, that features some of the bests contemporary photographers.
-pp. 80-83

George Strouzas
www.be.net/GeorgeStrouzas

George Strouzas lives and works in Athens (Greece) as a graphic designer. He studied Graphic Design at AKTO art & design College and gained his BA (honours) degree from the Middlesex University of London. He loves street art and Swiss graphic design from the 50's till today, a letter lover. He loves design, especially typography, as well as type

creation. He loves to collaborate with people abroad and share culture and design technics.
-pp. 66-67

Glasfurd & Walker
www.glasfurdandwalker.com

Glasfurd & Walker is a creative studio specialising in ideation, graphic design and artisitic direction. The studio works with an international client base in a range of industries including, design, media, music, fashion, food & wine, the arts, cultural development, corporate and environmental. The studios services include identity & brand design, graphic design, art direction for print and online communication, exhibition, installation and packaging.
-pp. 36-37

Graphics Designed
www.jackcrossing.com

Born and raised just outside of London Jack has always been involved in some sort of creative field. After graduating from Bath spa University in 2008 jack set up GRAPHICS DESIGNED as a platform for his freelance work. Primarily working with typography GRAPHICS DESIGNED is always looking for new methods of creative production.
-p. 105

Guilherme Falcão
www.guilhermefalcao.com

Guilherme Falcão Pelegrino is a graphic designer from São Paulo, Brazil. He achieved a BA from the Senac College of Communication and Arts in 2006 and is currently a postgraduate student of Art: Critique and Curating at PUC/COGEAE (2011). His activities as a designer also include workshops, lectures, collaborations, self initiated projects such as the Parasite Zine and Pequeno Comitê, a think tank of cultural projects and ideas. His works have been featured in books and publications both inside and outside of Brazil.
-pp. 102-103, 114-115

Gunmad
www.gunmad.net

Gunmad is the collaborative name of the 2 graphic designers, Guðmundur Ingi Úlfarsson and Mads Freund Brunse. They originally started their collaboration in Denmark, but later went on to finish their studies in The Netherlands and Switzerland. They are currently located between these three countries and Iceland.
-pp. 106-109

Joe Hinder
www.joehinder.co.uk

Freelance Graphic Designer living and working in London, England.
-pp. 122-125

Jonas Wandeler for Graphic Thought Facility
www.jonaswandeler.ch
www.graphicthoughtfacility.com

After attending the foundation year in his hometown of Fribourg/Switzerland, Jonas Wandeler went on to study visual communication at the Zurich Academy of the Arts. Looking for some work experience, he turned to London for internships in the studios of GTF and Value and Service. His path then lead him to the Rietveld Academy in Amsterdam, where he graduated in 2010. Besides school projects he has been working with different cultural institutions like the Neue Galerie in Bern or the concert venue Bad Bonn.
-pp. 44-45

Julien Arts&Maarten van Gent
www.julienarts.nl
www.maartenvangent.nl

What started of as a playful way of reacting on each other's work and/or combining their different styles now functions as a way to visually map and expand their network. The DADA design method "Cadavre Exquis" became the starting point of visual conversation between

THEM and the people they love to work with. By working together on a canvas with seeing just a glimpse of what the other is doing, the outcome can be very surprising and challenging on the boundaries of graphic design itself. Because it can be used on different kinds of canvasses (still/motion/text/acting) the method creates an infinite set of chances and new creative opportunities.
- pp. 76-77

kokokumaru
www.kokokumaru.com

Yoshimaru Takahashi is a graphic designer and the president of Kokokumaru Inc. He is a visiting professor of the Osaka University of Art Graduate school. Yoshimaru is a member of JAGDA, Tokyo-TDC, NYTDC, JTA. Japanese culture and communication has a deep impact on him. His work focuses on typography design and got an international reputation. He has won many awards, as the Silver Award at New York A D C, Bronze Prize at N Y Festival and Judges Choice at Asia Graphics Awards.
-pp. 148-151

L2M3 Kommunikationsdesign
www.L2M3.com

L2M3 Kommunikationsdesign is a graphic design agency with high standards of form and content. Founded by Sascha Lobe in 1999, the agency handles signage systems and graphic design for exhibitions in addition to traditional tasks such as developing corporate images and designing printed matter. So far, the agency has received more than 100 international awards in all areas of visual communication, e.g. at the red dot, iF Award, the European Design Award, and the Type Directors Club New York. Sascha Lobe is a member of the Alliance Graphique Internationale (AGI) and professor for typography at HfG Offenbach.
-pp. 112-113

of Convent Garden, they create memorable visual communications that engage target audiences, build brands and achieve business results. Ragged Edge Design's work is strategic, innovative and successful. You can come to them for logos and identities, websites and e-commerce, digital marketing, print design and brand strategy.
-pp. 30-31

ruiz+company
www.ruizcompany.com

A Studio of art directors and Designers, Ruiz + Company create branding, communication, packaging and advertising for a range of international clients, across fashion, manufacturing and retail. Featured in countless books and magazines, and winning more than 100 awards, David Ruiz is a respected member of the International design community.
-pp. 38-41

StudioSpass
www.studiospass.com

StudioSpass (fun studio) is: Jaron Korvinus & Daan Mens. Since April 2008, they run an office for visual communication in the heart of Rotterdam, The Netherlands. They specialized in making campaigns and visual identities, both in print and in pixels. StudioSpass is evolving into an all round design office. They avoid being trapped into corners and fixed formulae, and really value Spass and passion in design. StudioSpass: "Appreciation to us is hearing from our clients that they recognize the Spass we have in our work."
-pp. 140-143

Superatelier
www.superatelier.com

Superatelier is a small graphic design studio based in the south of France. They do print work (posters, brochures, etc.), as well as a bit of web design, mostly for arts and culture clients. Anna was born and bred in Montpellier. After her studies at EPSAA in Paris, she decided to come back to work in the south. Her specialities are layouts (print and web), photography and lasagnas. Mathieu is from Senlis and is also a graduate from EPSAA. He creates beautiful posters and visual identities, and practices skateboarding. « It's all about balance » he confided.
-pp. 110-111

SuperBruut
www.superbruut.nl

SuperBruut is... the most original, the idealist, the visionary, the number one and that guy who was, with his eight years, left behind at a rest stop along the Belgian highway. These things are not all completely true, except for the last... Yes he is that guy who was standing on a rest stop crying. That guy who was picked up by the police. That guy who sat for four hours on the Belgian police station. That guy who was spoiled by the police with soda cans and chocolate bars. These days that guy doesn't get left behind along the Belgian highway. Nowadays that guy designs. He is Thijs... He is that guy.
-pp. 54, 68-69, 78-79

underbau
www.underbau.com

Underbau is a project which came came to life by the union of Juanjo Justicia and Joaquín Labayen in 2008, two freelance designers with years of experience in the field of publishing, corporate and advertising design. From the very beginning, the studio activity has been linked to art and culture, working in both national and international projects from institutions such as Instituto Cervantes, the Culture Department of the Andalusian Government, the Scientific Research Council or the Sport Council. Underbau's work is based on efficiency and design coherence, taking control of the whole creative process, from the initial conceptualization to the final production.
-pp. 132-133

The Click Design
www.theclickdesign.com

The Click Design Consultants is an award-winning, independent, multi-disciplined creative design consultancy. We create outstanding brands. It's our passion. Developing engaging, memorable and effective work audiences really click with – we focus on brand identity, advertising, print and digital communications.
-pp. 72-73

thisislove studio
www.thisislove.pt

thisislove is a Lisbon based independent design studio founded in 2007. From Communication Design to experimental media projects, one of our main objectives is to create a multidisciplinary platform. Our projects question the process of creation and interaction between people, objects and signs. We make ideas real, with a great eye for detail and hidden meanings, developing quality outcomes. thisislove works in collaboration with other designers, architects, curators, fashion artists, photographers, marketing strategists, and many other individual talents.
-pp. 42-43

TwoPoints.Net
www.twopoints.net

TwoPoints.Net was founded in 2007 with the aim to do exceptional design work. Work that is tailored to the client's needs, work that excites the client's customers, work that hasn't been done before, work that does more than work. The market immediately responded to such an offer. In only a few years TwoPoints.Net have been able to compile a set of very diverse, high quality projects. TwoPoints.Net is a small company that thinks big. Not just in terms of international clientele, but with their network as well. This network includes musicians, photographers, software developers and writers, among many others. The core of TwoPoints.Net's network is directed by Lupi Asensio and Martin Lorenz, two graphic designers with German, Dutch and Spanish education and experience.
-pp. 90-97

Why Not Associates
www.whynotassociates.com

On leaving the Royal College of Art in 1987 Andy formed the multi disciplinary design group Why Not Associates with fellow graduates Howard Greenhalgh and David Ellis. In over 20 years of experience Andy has worked on projects ranging from exhibition design to postage stamps via advertising, publishing, television titles, commercials, corporate identity and public art. Why Not Associates clients include the Royal Academy of Arts, Malcolm Mcclaren, Pompidou Centre, Royal Mail, Nike, Paul Smith, Virgin Records, Antony Gormley, BBC, Channel 4 and the Tate Modern.
Andrew John Altmann
Born 16.09.62.
BA Hons Graphic Design – Central Saint Martins 1982 to 1985
MA Graphic Design – Royal College of Art 1985 to 1987
-pp. 52-53

First published and distributed by
viction:workshop ltd.

viction:ary™

Unit C, 7th Floor, Seabright Plaza,
9-23 Shell Street, North Point, Hong Kong
URL: www.victionary.com
Email: we@victionary.com

Designed & Edited by TwoPoints.Net
— The TwoPoints.Net team that worked on this book:
Martin Lorenz, Lupi Asensio, Juanra Pastor Rovira, Cornelia Brezing,
Judith Will and Natalie Birkle.

Interview with Albert-Jan Pool by Martin Lorenz

Fonts in I Love DIN:
FF DIN Pro Medium
FF DIN Pro Medium Italic
FF DIN Pro Bold
FF DIN Pro Bold Italic

Kindly supplied by Jürgen Siebert of FontShop International.

©2011 viction:workshop ltd.

ISBN 978-988-19438-9-7

The captions and artwork in this book are based on material supplied
by the designers whose work is included. While every effort has been
made to ensure their accuracy, viction:workshop does not under any
circumstances accept any responsibility for any errors or omissions.

Printed and bound in China

We would like to thank all the designers and companies who made
significant contribution to the compilation of this book. Without them
this project would not be able to accomplish. We would also like to
thank all the producers for their invaluable assistance throughout
this entire proposal. The successful completion also owes a great
deal to many professionals in the creative industry who have given us
precious insights and comments. We are also very grateful to many
other people whose names did not appear on the credits but have
made specific input and continuous support the whole time.